Did you know that
there are single words for . . .

- the delusion that one is beautiful?
- the sensation caused by tickling?
- the fear of one's mother-in-law?
- a witty retort you wish you had said but
  thought of too late?

You'll find them all—and much, much more—
in *Weird Words* . . . an incredible collection of
unique, unusual and useful words that will
provide hours of enjoyment *and* a vocabulary
lesson like you've never had before!

WEIRD WORDS

WEIRD WORDS

Irwin M. Berent and Rod L. Evans

BERKLEY BOOKS, NEW YORK

WEIRD WORDS

A Berkley Book / published by arrangement with
the authors

PRINTING HISTORY
Berkley edition / March 1995

All rights reserved.
Copyright © 1995 by Irwin M. Berent and Rod L. Evans.
This book may not be reproduced in whole or in part,
by mimeograph or any other means, without permission.
For information address: The Berkley Publishing Group,
200 Madison Avenue, New York, New York 10016.

ISBN: 0-425-14404-6

BERKLEY®
Berkley Books are published by The Berkley Publishing Group,
200 Madison Avenue, New York, New York 10016.
BERKLEY and the "B" design
are trademarks belonging to Berkley Publishing Corporation.

PRINTED IN THE UNITED STATES OF AMERICA

10 9 8 7 6 5 4 3 2 1

Contents

Introduction

It's a funny thing, the English language. We have perhaps over a million words from which to choose. And each word has its own charm and beauty, its own color and texture, so that if one word is not precisely suitable or does not express the precise idea or feeling, there is almost always another word that will, the variety in our language being so great. There are in fact so many words that no single dictionary can contain all of them, and— here's the irony—we often can't find a good word with which to express ourselves.

A result is that we have even come to think that there *are* no words to denote a number of quite common situations and issues. For example, how many people believe that there actually is a single word for "the tendency to forget names" or for "one who never laughs" or for "lasting two days" or for "causing a myth to arise" or for "the adult imitation of baby talk"?

Well, believe it or not, there is a single word for each of those phrases. They are, respectively: "lethonomia," "agelast," "biduous," "mythopoeic," and "hypocorism." We call such words "unique" because they are essentially the only ones that denote what they're denoting. In other words, they have no synonyms. We've coined the term "insynonymable" (insinuhNIMable) to mean "having no synonyms." In effect, you will not find any word in this book whose meaning could be represented with any other single popularly known word. For example, "cynosure" ("a person or thing that is a center of attention") would require at least three other words—"center of attention"—to express the same idea; there is no common one-word synonym for "cynosure." (You could, of course, use the word "center," but it would not adequately capture the meaning of "cynosure.")

This dictionary contains some of the most fascinating words in the English language, *many* of which are insynonymable and most of which have, until now, been remarkably difficult for anyone to find. In addition, the Thesauro-Index, designed especially for this dictionary, helps make these words particularly easy for readers to find. (To learn how to get the most use from the Thesauro-Index, see "How to Use this Book.")

How Can Rare Words Be Used?

You're probably thinking now, "But if these words have been so difficult to find, and if, therefore, few people know their meanings, then how can I use the words without utterly baffling the person to whom I'm speaking or writing?"

Of course, some of you may *like* to baffle others, either because you want to show people that you know something that they don't or because you want them to suspect—incorrectly—that they have been insulted. For example, to someone who has just removed his shoes, you might say, "I'm surprised to see that you've just discalceated in front of me." Doubtless, though, your "victims" will be sufficiently puzzled or provoked sim-

2

ply to ask you what the word means. And at that point you can choose either to enlighten them or leave them shaking in their boots (or, in their feet, if they're discalceated).

There are, however, less sadistic and pompous ways to make effective use of rare words. The fact is, you can use rare words so that they require practically no explanation to be understood. Consider, for example, this sentence in which it is reasonably obvious that the word "androcracy" probably relates to "government by men":

This government is closer to an androcracy than a democracy, since it contains virtually all men.

And this sentence, in which "emacity" ("an itch to be buying") is used:

When she goes on a shopping spree her emacity is out of control—she's got an itch to be buying and that's how she scratches it.

You can also use the words instructively, as when you say or write:

He knows a great deal about every field—that is, he's a real polymath.

or:

You must hate waiting in long lines; in other words, you've got macrophobia.

Note that the word order—that is, the syntax—above is less likely to be interpreted as condescending than the reverse order.

He is a real polymath—that is, he knows a great deal about every field.

or:

You've got macrophobia—that is, a condition of fearing long waits.

If the person to whom you're speaking already knows what those words mean, those two sentences might sound condescending.

At times, the physical surroundings will provide enough clues to enable your listener to grasp your meaning quite clearly. For example, as you hand someone a pair of nail-clippers while pointing to the person's fingernails, you might say, "Perhaps this will help you exungulate."

Finally, if your listener is still baffled, there is always the following alternative—a special favorite of ours, for obvious reasons: "Look it up in Berent and Evans." Indeed, once this book becomes a best-seller, many of its words might fall into common usage, and soon everyone will be using them. (Hey, we can dream, can't we?)

Why Aren't These Words Used More Often?

Perhaps one reason why many of the words in this dictionary have not fallen into common usage is that their usefulness is often not readily apparent. But the words here have been selected not merely because they are unique but also because they lend themselves to either literal or figurative use. In other words, some of these words may have only very narrow usefulness when they're used literally. The word "filipendulous," for example, could be used literally only when referring to something hanging by an actual thread. But even though its literal use is limited, imaginative writers and speakers can come up with a number of quite colorful and illustrative figurative uses for a word like "filipendulous." If you were writing about someone who'll be fired if he makes another, however slight, error, you might say that the person's "filipendulous state of employment is becoming more in doubt by the minute."

Or consider the word "antisigogglin," which means "tilted to the left." Although it's a useful word to designate a direction, it can also easily be converted to political use: "Although American politics was decidedly antisigogglin in the 1960s and 1970s, the Reagan presidency moved the country back toward the right."

Numerous other words could be used figuratively, too. For example, "infarct" ("an area of dead tissue") could be applied to anywhere that is desolate or forsaken, "galanty" ("a puppet show") could be applied to any instance in which one person is controlling another, and "sypher" ("to join edge to edge to form an even surface") could be applied to bringing together dissimilar people with different ideas to produce creative solutions. And the list could go on and on. . . .

Taken as a whole, the words in this dictionary should make for entertaining reading. You may, for example, be delightfully surprised at times to find words that describe things for which you would have doubted there were words. For example, "infucation"—the act of putting on makeup—is a great word when applied figuratively to "putting a good face on" any problematic situation.

This dictionary should be as useful to writers as it will be entertaining to word-lovers (logophiles, that is). Open it anywhere and enjoy!

How to Use This Book

You can use this dictionary in two main ways. One is simply to pick it up and start reading. At almost any page you may find a number of fascinating words that you never knew existed. If, however, you want to find a word for a specific subject, you'll want first to refer to the Thesauro-Index at the end of this book.

Using the Thesauro-Index

Now think of a word that generally describes the subject in which you're interested, and then look up that topic word in the Thesauro-Index. There you'll find a list of specific words to which to refer in the dictionary (or you'll be directed to see another topic word instead).

For example, if you want to find words related to air, you'll look up "AIR" and find four words ("aerobic," "leeward," "sortie," and "triphibious") listed under that topic that you can then look up in the main dictionary. If you looked under, say, "WIND" rather than "AIR," the Thesauro-Index will tell you to "See AIR."

Suppose, however, that after looking up each of the four words, you find that none of them is quite the one that you need. You can now use the Thesauro-Index much as you would use an ordinary thesaurus; under each topic word, you'll find a list of other related categories to consult. In the present example, you would return to the Thesauro-Index topic-word "AIR" and find the following:

AIR (see also AIRPLANE, BREATHING, COVER-
ING [AS IN CLOUD], SMELL, SMOKING, STAR,
SUN)
aerobic, leeward, sortie, triphibious

You can then consult one or a few of those topic words as well. Suppose you decide, for example, that "SMELL" may be a useful topic word. You look it up in the Thesauro-Index and then consult the words suggested under that topic word. Still not satisfied? Then return to the "SMELL" topic word in the Thesauro-Index and see what other topic words are suggested.

SMELL (see also AIR, BREATHING, FEELING,
GOOD/BAD [AS IN STENCH], NOSE)
mephitis, olid

Some of the topic words suggested are the same as those suggested with the original topic word, but some are new topic-words: "FEELING," "GOOD/BAD," and "NOSE." The more topic words you consult, the further you will get into the shades and colors of meaning of the original idea for which you were searching. Thus, starting with words related to air, you may end up with "brevirostrate" ("having a short nose"), which is listed with two other words under the topic-word "NOSE."

So by using the Thesauro-Index you may discover a

whole universe of ideas and senses that your original word only begins to capture. Indeed, every topic word is followed by at least one cross-reference to another topic word, and some more general topic words carry ten or more cross-references. This means that you can begin with only the vaguest idea of the word you're seeking and be led to the most nearly precise and most colorful word for your needs. Often, in fact, a cross-reference is made to a figuratively related heading. For example, "mountains" carries a cross-reference to "problems." In the end, the word that you arrive at may represent anything from an exact description of a concrete object to a word that denotes a humorously abstract figurative idea.

Some Notes About the Definitions

Note that we do not usually specify whether the word entered is an adjective, noun, verb, or adverb. Remember that most definitions beginning with an "-ing" (or "-ed") word are definitions of adjectives (at least, this is true for this dictionary); those beginning with "a," "the," "one who," "-tion" words, and so on are usually definitions of nouns; those beginning with "to" are verbs; and those beginning with "by," "for," "with," and so on are adverbs.

Note also that we have not always given all the possible definitions for each word entered but only those definitions or parts of definitions that are most colorful, useful, and unusual.

A Note on Pronunciation and Word Origins

We've provided the pronunciations of most words whose pronunciations might be in doubt. We've also explained the roots of many headwords, especially those that are unusual or otherwise interesting.

We have provided only a brief explanation of the meanings and origins of the roots, however—not a detailed etymological analysis. Where a related word is defined within one of these root explanations, we have given only a partial definition that is immediately pertinent to the root in question. Finally, where an ancient, or Indo-European, root is presented, keep in mind that these "ultimate," or original, roots are very often based on speculation—that is, etymologists have concluded that a

CAPitalized LETters INdicate ACcented PORtion of word		
ā = late	**bird/**	s = sit
a = pat	**turn**	sh = show
aw = **awe** / **bar**	g = get	th = thin
/**bought**	ī = bike	*th* = the
ch = **child**	i = pit	u = but / pull
ch = German	j = joy	*u* = boot
"ch"	ō = rope	' = very short
ē = Pete	o = pot	"uh"
e = pet	*oi* - **oil** / **boy**	• = for pause
er = **water/**	*ow* = **out** / **cow**	or clarifica-
word/	*or* = bore	tion

root pronounced roughly a certain way is most likely the source of a particular word. In almost every instance, of course, this "original" word preceded written history and has, therefore, not been found.

Dictionary

A

ab irato   (ob ēROtō)   not to be taken seriously

"The remarks of angry people must not be taken seriously but rather **ab irato**."

"Ab irato" is a Latin expression meaning, literally, "from an angry man." For generally what comes from an angry man is often exaggerated, unclear, and irrational, and therefore often "not to be taken seriously."

You might think, then, that "irato" is related in origin to the word "irrational," since people often behave irrationally when they are angry. In fact, though, the word originates, not from "irrational," but from the same root as other words directly related to anger—for example, "irate," "ire," and "irascible." Those words all stem from the original Indo-European root, *eis*, which meant to "set in fast motion," which in turn suggests "great power." In fact, another *ir*-word, "iron," comes directly from the Germanic "**ei**sen," and indeed iron is a powerful—that is, strong—metal.

abbozzo   (uB*AW*Tsō)   a rough draft or sketch

"The student agreed to give the teacher an **abbozzo** to ensure that the topic was appropriate."

The *bozzo* part of this word comes directly from the Italian word *bozza,* which means "swelling." It is also the root of "emboss." Embossing might involve creating a raised ornament by carving—in effect, creating a protuberance, or swelling, if you will. So, to make an abbozzo in wood, rather than, say, on paper, you would have to carve out the letters or artwork, in a sense causing them to swell.

Abderian (abDIRēun)   pertaining to foolish or excessive laughter

"Their **Abderian** laughter annoyed their solemn hosts."

abecedarian (ābēsēDĀRēun)   a person learning or teaching the alphabet or the fundamentals of a subject

"We realize that our first-year engineering students are **abecedarians** who need to proceed slowly."

You might say that this is a pure onomatopoeic word, since it sounds precisely like what it pertains to: the ABCs.

aboiement (obwoMAWN)   the uncontrollable and involuntary production of abnormal or unusual sounds

"Even though we knew that he couldn't help himself, we couldn't resist laughing in response to the sounds produced by his **aboiement**."

aboral   away from the mouth

> "The animal's tail is so far from its mouth that it's
> about as **aboral** as any appendage could be."

The *or* part of this word has its roots in the original
Indo-European word *or*, which referred to the utterance
of a god. Hence, an "oracle" is the medium, such as a
priestess, through whom a deity transmits a response.
And "adore" (literally, "to pray to") originally referred to
speaking to—praying to, that is—one's deity or deities.
  Since one speaks through one's mouth, the "or" word
was incorporated in the Latin words *oris* and *os*, meaning
mouth or entrance. From that Latin root we have "oral,"
"orifice," and even "usher," which comes from the Latin
ustiarus (or *ostiarus*), literally "doorkeeper." The word
for "door," *ostium*, contains the original *os* root: for a
door is, after all, located at the opening, or mouth.
  For another ancestor of the *or/os* root, see "osculant."

acceptilation   (akseptuLĀshun)   free remission of li-
ability or debt

> "Through Jesus' merit and death, God, according to
> many Christians, has granted human beings **accep-
> tilation** for their sins."

accessit   (akSESit)   honorable mention of one who
comes nearest to a prize

> "Although she didn't win the prize, she was grati-
> fied to receive an **accessit**."

accismus (akSIZmus)   a pretended refusal or disclaiming, as when a guest rejects the host's initial offer of a drink in the hope that the host will insist that the guest have a drink, or when a politician insists that he or she has no plans to run for office while secretly hoping to be nominated

> "We believe that his first refusal is simply an **accismus**, designed to provoke us to ask again but with greater urgency."

accrescent (uKRESunt)   growing with age

> "At the rate that it's growing, my **accrescent** kitten will be as big as a lion by Christmas."

The *cre* part of this word is the root of a number of words associated with growth and growing, most of which originate from the Greek *khoros*, meaning "youth." Those words include "crescent" (the seemingly growing moon), "crescendo," "cereal" (grains, which are seeds), "creation," "creature," "increase," "decrease," "increment," "accrue," "concretion" (literally, a "growing together"), "crew" (originally "reinforcements"), and "recruit." For more about the root of these and other words, see "hypo**cor**ism," below.

acculturation   the condition of cultural change in one society being affected by another

> "No culture that regularly comes into contact with others can avoid some degree of **acculturation**; under those circumstances, influence is inevitable."

acupinge   to paint with a needle

"The artist used to **acupinge** but now prefers to paint with a brush."

acyrology   (as*er*OLujee)   poor choice of words

"When I said 'ain't' instead of 'isn't,' they accused me of **acyrology**."

ad ignorantiam   (ad ignōRONtēum)   the manner by which the truth of something is argued, usually by (a) relying on the hearer's ignorance of an essential fact, (b) maintaining that it is true because it has not been proved false, or (c) challenging another to disprove it rather than offering any proof of one's own

"They were arguing **ad ignorantiam** when they argued that ghosts must exist since no one has conclusively disproved their existence."

For information about the *gn* part of this word, see "gnomon."

ad libitum   (adLIButum)   as much or as long as desired

"You may criticize her position **ad libitum**, but she is committed to following it through."

adfenestrate   to sneak in through a window

"Burglars are more likely to **adfenestrate** than to enter through the front door."

adiabolism (ādiABuliz′m) the condition of not believing in the devil

"She was more offended by his atheism than by his **adiabolism**, since she herself at times had doubts about the devil's existence."

The "devil" is "diabolic." Indeed, in French, the word for "devil" is *diable*; in Italian, *diavolo*; in Spanish, *diablo*; and in Swedish, *djavul*. The word "devil" comes from the Greek word *diabolus*, meaning literally "slanderer." *Diabolus* in turn, comes from two ancient roots, *dia*, meaning "through," and *ballein*, meaning "to throw." The idea is that the devil throws (a curve ball?) through people.

The same *ball* or *bol* root is in "sym**bol**" (literally, "to throw together"; ideas or signs thrown together), "em**bl**em" (literally, "thrown on"), and "para**ble**" (from "para**ball**ein," "to throw beside": a fictitious story that illustrates—or is thrown beside—a real-life situation or moral problem). Finally, "pro**bl**em" is itself from a word meaning "to throw, or put, forward." Indeed, problems often seem to throw themselves in our way to baffle and confuse us.

advesperate (adVESperāt) to draw toward evening

"As the day **advesperated**, it began to get dark."

The *vesper* part of this word comes from the Indo-European root *wes-pero*, meaning "evening" or "night."

From "wes," we have the English word "**west**." The **Visi**goths were western Goths. "Vesper" is the evening star. In botany, "**vesper**tine" describes flowers that open or bloom in the evening, and in zoology, "vespertine" describes animals such as bats and owls that are active at night.

aegrotat   (Ēgrōtat)   a student's written medical excuse

"The teacher didn't require the student who was ill to hand in an **aegrotat**, but she did want him to get the notes he missed from another student."

aerobic   (uRŌBik)   growing only in the presence of oxygen; also that which lives in the air

"Fire is in a sense **aerobic**, since it cannot exist in the absence of oxygen."

afterages   (AFter • ājiz)   a child born long after its siblings

"She is an **afterages** who was born more than twenty years after her brother and sister."

afterimage   a sensation of color experienced after the stimulus has been removed, as when a bright image is seen after closing the eyes (called a "positive afterimage")

"After she saw the bright lights, she saw an **after-image**."

agastopia   (Aguh • STŌPēu)   admiration of a particular part of someone's body

"All eyes were fixed on the bodybuilder's massive arms as if everyone in the room displayed a collective **agastopia**."

agate   (Agut)   a measurement of advertising space

agathism   belief that everything works toward ultimate good, no matter what the short-term consequences; the concept that all is for the better

"I realize that things don't look good for you now, but I subscribe to **agathism** and believe that things will ultimately be for the good."

agelast   one who never laughs

"Be careful about relying on **agelasts** for sympathy, since those who don't laugh won't be able to uplift you."

agnogenic   (agnōJENik)   of unknown cause

"The doctor believes that one day we'll find the cause of the currently **agnogenic** disease."

For information about the *gn* and *gen* parts of this word, see "gnomon."

agonal   (Agunul)   a tale of suffering and death, or the agony of death itself

"Religious people try to find meaning in **agonals**."

agowilt   (Aguwilt)   sickening or sudden fear

"He experienced **agowilt** as soon as he realized that
the reason he couldn't find his car in the parking lot
might be that it had been stolen."

agroof   (aGR*U*F)   flat on one's face

"She was most likely pushed from behind, since she
landed **agroof**."

agyiophobia   (AJēōFŌBēu)   fear of crossing busy
streets

"He claimed that he didn't have **agyiophobia** but
simply a prudent concern to avoid being run over."

aha experience   the moment of insight or realization of
a solution to a problem

"When she saw the key to solving the math problem, she had an **aha experience**."

aheliotropic   (uHĒlēuTROPik)   tending to turn away
from light

"Contrary to popular belief, some plants are **aheliotropic**."

The main roots of this word are *a* (not), *helio* (sun, or
light), and *trop* (turn).

21

Helio comes from the Indo-European word for "sun": *sauel* or *suen*. One can see how *sauel* could ultimately give English its *sol* words ("solar," "parasol," etc.) as well as "south." And one can see how *suen* became "sun." How *sauel* gave us "helio" is less obvious: apparently, *sauel-yo* became *helios*, the name of the sun god of Olympus. Remember that "s," "sh," and "h" are related linguistically. (See also "aphelion.")

algometer (alGOMut*er*) instrument measuring sensitivity to pain

"We didn't need an **algometer** to know that he was in a great deal of pain."

algon a unit of pain

"Stepping on that nail caused him to feel several **algons**."

allotheism (ALuthēiz′m) worship of strange gods

"Although Socrates was accused of **allotheism**, he denied worshiping any foreign or unsanctioned gods."

The *allo* part of this word means "other" (hence, "strange"). The root originates from the Indo-European root *al*, which meant "beyond" or "other." That root appears in the other *allo-* words below as well as in "par**all**el" (literally, "beside one another"), "**all**ergy" (literally, "working otherwise"—that is, reacting abnormally), "**al**ias" (another name), "**al**ien" (from some other place), "**al**ibi" (literally, "other," or "elsewhere"—that is, an excuse that one was elsewhere than at a crime scene), "**al**ternate," "**al**truism" (regard for **others**), "**ul**tra-" words (beyond), "**ul**terior," "**ul**timate" (beyond to the farthest or final), "ad**ul**terate" (to put one thing with another—that is, to pollute or defile), "outrage" (from "**ou**tre," meaning "beyond, in excess"), and "else."

allotrope (ALutrōp)   the form taken by an allotropic element

"Graphite is an **allotrope** of carbon."

allotropy (ALutrōpē)   existence of an element in more than one form (adjective: allotropic)

"Carbon, sulfur, and phosphorous are known for their **allotropy**, since they exist in two or more distinct forms."

alpinist (ALpunist)   a mountain climber

"When Robert Kennedy climbed Mount Kennedy, he was with some highly experienced **alpinists**."

amathophobia   fear of dust

"His **amathophobia** prompted him to carry mops and dustcloths everywhere."

anacoluthon (anukuL*U*thon)   a switch from one syntactical construction, left incomplete, to another in the same sentence, as in "I can't believe that you— Oh, forget it!"

"Her **anacoluthon** hid her seething irritation with what she considered stupidity on the part of her friend."

"Anacoluthon" comes from the Greek word for "not following," in the sense of "not being logical"—as in "It doesn't follow." It is illogical to say the opposite of what you start out saying.

The *caluthu* part of this word originates from the Indo-European root *kel*, which meant "to speed, drive." In a sense, one's logica is driven along a path on which it follows. *Kel* appears in "ac**cel**erate" and even "**cel**ebrate." (*Celebris* is Latin for "of a crowded place"—in other words, a place whose paths many people walk frequently and rapidly. Hence, if a place is very popular, it might logically be a famous, or celebrated, place.)

Ultimately even the word "hold" originates from the *kel* root. Remember that "k," "ch," and "h" are all related, so that the Indo-European *kel* could become Germanic "**hol**d." And what do speed and driving have to do with holding? Well, the original idea of driving, as in driving cattle, was extended to the idea of tending, and finally actually to possessing, or holding, something— cattle or anything else.

anadramous (uNADrumus) swimming upstream, especially to spawn

"Shad and salmon are **anadramous** and must therefore move up from the sea to rivers to spawn."

anagoge (ANugōjē)   spiritual and mystical interpretations of words

"He doesn't think much of **anagoge** but prefers a straightforward interpretation of scripture."

anamorphosis (anuMORFusis)   a distorted image recognizable only through an appropriate device; in biology, evolution by slow changes

"The theologian was insisting that the image that we human beings have of God is an **anamorphosis**, distorted by our human experiences, prejudices, and other limitations and clarified only occasionally by faith and grace."

androcracy (anDROKrusē)   government headed by men

"No feminist is going to aprove of an **androcracy**."

androlepsy (ANdrulepsē)   the seizure of citizens of one nation by the government of another nation (exemplified especially during the Iran crisis)

"The speaker said that **androlepsy** is nothing more than government-sanctioned kidnapping and that it should be unconditionally condemned."

anhedonia (anhēDŌNēu)   the inability to experience pleasure

"A person who has **anhedonia** doesn't take pleasure in even those activities that he or she usually likes."

Hedone is the Greek word for "pleasure," from which arises the word "hedonist" and other *hedo* words. The original root is from the Indo-European *suad,* meaning "sweet" or "pleasant." The *suad* root gave rise not only to the Greek *hedone* but also to the Latin *suadere*, which in turn spawned the English words "sweet" and "persuade" (by offering sweet talk, one can often successfully persuade).

At first glance, it may not seem that the Latin *suadere* and the Greek *hedone* would be related, since one begins with an "s" and the other, "h." Keep in mind, though, that a number of Latin roots beginning with "s" have the same meanings as Greek roots beginning with "h." For example, both *septa-* (Latin origin) and *hepta-* (Greek origin) mean "seven," and both *somno-* (Latin) and *hypno-* (Greek) mean "sleep."

For another example of a *hedon-* word, see "nikhedonia."

anililagnia (anī • liLAGnēu) a young man's erotic interest in a much older woman

"According to some viewers, young Harold's interest in the much older Maude illustrates the power of **anililagnia**, whereas other viewers regard the relationship as strange but nonsexual."

The *lagnia* part of "anililagnia" comes from the Greek *lagneia*, meaning "lust." Thus, "urolagnia" refers to sexual excitement associated with urine, "algolagnia" refers to sexual excitement associated with pain, and "melolagnia" . . . well, you can guess, or look it up in this dictionary.

"Anile" means "of or like an old woman," coming from the Latin word for "old woman," "anus."

anisosthenic   (anĪSos • THENik)   of unequal strength

> "The huge weight lifter and his frail young son are obviously **anisosthenic**."

The *iso* part of this word means "equal." A simple way to remember what *iso* means is simply to consider that "is" means "equals" and that in expressing simple math problems, "equals" and "is" are often used interchangeably—for example, "two plus two *equals* four" or "two plus two *is* four."

anoesis   (anōĒsis)   in psychology, mere reception of impressions without intellectual effort

> "Some mystics believe that their apprehension of the world as a limited whole is an **anoesis**, which would be distorted by trying to understand it by using our ordinary intellectual categories."

antipluvial   preventing precipitation

> "We need the opposite of a rain dance; we need an **antipluvial** dance."

The *pluv* part of this word comes from the original Indo-European root, *pleu*, which meant "flow." In Greek

27

mythology, the lord of the underworld and of all the treasures of the earth was called **Plu**to, or Plutodores, because everything **flowed** from him. And in Roman myth, Jupiter **Plu**vius reigned over the heavens, having the power to bring rain and thunder.

By a linguistic process called metathesis, in which certain letters are reversed, the original *pleu* root also became *pulmo*, a root meaning "lungs" (it was observed that the lungs of a plucked fowl floated when thrown into water, while the other organs sank).

Finally, "pl" became "fl" ("p," "ph," and "f" are all related sounds), and a number of other words related to flowing—including "flow" itself—became part of English—for example, "flea," "fleet," "flight," "float," "flotsam," "flutter," "fly," "fowl" (from *flug*, which, by metathesis, became *fugl*), and even "fletcher"—one who makes arrows, which flow through the air.

For other *pleu* roots, see "fugleman."

antipodal (anTIPudul) opposite, especially pertaining to locations on the globe

"Although they lived thousands of miles away from each other in **antipodal** latitudes, they were remarkably similar philosophically."

antipudic (antiPY*U*dik) that which covers the private parts of the body

"In many artistic depictions of Eve, a fig leaf functions as an **antipudic**."

antiscians (anTISH′nz) people living on the same meridian but on different sides of the equator, so that they cast shadows at noon in opposite directions

> "From an objective point of view, **antiscians** can't argue that anyone is upside down on earth."

antisigogglin (anti • siGOGlin) tilted to the left

> "He wanted to know whether the Eiffel Tower tilts to the right or whether, like liberal Democrats, it is **antisigogglin**."

antistasis (anTIStusis) the defense of an action that claims the action prevented something worse from happening

> "While few Americans thought that the dropping of the A-bombs was a positive good, they thought that it could be defended as an **antistasis**."

aphasia (uFĀZyu) loss of the power to use words

> "One thing the voluble Robin Williams has never had to worry about is **aphasia**."

Not surprisingly, the root for the word meaning "speak" is interspersed in a number of English words that are sometimes quite differently spelled. All those words, however, share one simple origin: Indo-European *bha*, meaning "speak." From it, we have "a**pha**sia" as well as "blas**phe**my" ("evil-speaking"), "eu**phe**mism" ("good-speaking"), "tele**pho**ne" (from Greek *phone*, meaning "sound"), "infant" ("not speaking"), "affable" (easy to speak to), "ineffable" (inexpressible with speech), "fable," "defame," "famous" (that which has been well spoken of), "prophet," "professor," "confession," "preface" (from "praefari," meaning "to say before-hand"), and even "blame" (ultimately from Greek, *blasphemos*).

aphelion (aFĒLyun) point farthest from the sun

"If the sun represents the truth, then these fools have surely reached the **aphelion**."

For information about the *heli* part of this word, see "aheliotropic."

aphilophrenia (uFILōFRĒNēu) a feeling that one is unloved or unwanted

"The psychologist held that active people with strong self-esteem are less likely to feel **aphilophrenia** than passive people with weak self-esteem, since the latter are more likely to seek validation of their worth from others."

apistia (uPIStēu) faithlessness in marriage

"Only well after John F. Kennedy's death did the American public—as distinguished from many members of the press—know about his **apistia**."

apopemptoclinic (APō·pemptōKLINik) inclined toward divorce

"Although the marriage might survive this rough period, the husband's flagrant lack of consideration for his wife makes us believe that he is **apopemptoclinic**."

apophasis   (uPOFusis)   affirming something by denying it

"By saying that it would be unfair of her to bring up his 'indiscretions and lies,' she had executed a masterly **apophasis**."

arcifinious   (*aw*rsuFINēus)   having a border that forms a natural barrier, as from invasion

"Switzerland has usually been safe from invaders, largely because of its **arcifinious** terrain."

arenicolous   (aruNIKulus)   living in sand

"The sand crab is a good example of an **arenicolous** creature."

areology   (arēOLujē), **polemology**   the study of war

"The battles of Alexander the Great are part of any **areology**."

argot   (*AW*Rgō)   the vocabulary and idioms of a particular class or group of people, especially for private communication

"The FBI infiltrator had to learn the **argot** of criminals to sound convincing."

aristology (ariSTOLujē)   luncheon talk

"Although I usually enjoy listening to the **aristology** of my talkative luncheon partners, today I'll have to skip lunch."

The *arist* part of this word is actually two roots: *a* ("not") and *rist* ("fast"), the idea being that dining is *not fasting*. The *rist*, the word "fast," and the root *sito-* (which means "food" and which is found, for example, in "sitomania" below) are all based on the Indo-European root *past*, meaning "firm."

What does firmness have to do with fasting? In certain religious practices, the devout hold *firm*—hold fast, that is—on holy days by going without food—fasting. Further, a breakfast is literally a breaking of the previous night's fast.

armentose (*aw*rmenTŌS)   rich in animals or herds

"The wealthy rancher had an **armentose** spread."

armipotent (*aw*rMIPutent)   strong in arms; possessing powerful weapons

"Former President Ronald Reagan held that only **armipotent** nations are in a position to prevent wars."

arrhenotoky (aruNOTukē)   the bearing of male offspring only

"The mother's **arrhenotoky** became well known after every one of her male children became famous."

artuate (*AWR*chu • āt) to tear limb from limb

"According to 2 Kings 2:23–24, two bears **artuated** forty-two smart-alecky children."

atavistic reverting to or suggesting the characteristics of a remote ancestor or a primitive or earlier type

"He finds animal sacrifice repellent and **atavistic**."

The *atavist* part of this word comes from the Latin *ativus*, meaning "ancestor." The origin of *ativus* (literally, "father's grandfather") is in turn *atta* (baby talk for **daddy**) plus *avus* ("grandfather"). *Avus* is related to "**avu**ncular" and "**u**ncle."

auscultate (*AWS*cultāt) to examine by listening, as with a stethoscope

"The young girl wanted to use the stethoscope so that she could **auscultate** her own heart."

autarchia (*aw*TAW*Rkēu*) perpetual happiness

"A beer, a soda, a cigarette, a basketball game on TV—for a growing number of Americans, that's **autarchia**, at least until their team loses."

autarky state of national self-sufficiency

"We must achieve **autarky** so that our nation needn't be crippled every time OPEC nations raise the price of oil."

autophobia   fear of oneself or of being alone

"Since he suffered from **autophobia**, he constantly sought companionship."

autophonomania   (*aw*tō • fōnō • MĀNyu)   preoccupation with suicide

"**Autophonomania** is often a serious warning that a suicide could occur, so that those appearing to be obsessed with suicide ought to be taken seriously."

azoth   (Az*aw*th),   **panpharmacon, panacea**   an all-purpose medicine

"I don't believe in **azoths**, since so many diseases are, at least for now, incurable, and medicines usually have a highly specific range of application."

B

baraesthesia (b*aw*resTHEEzyu) the ability to perceive pressure

"She has an emotional **baraesthesia**, by which she can discern tensions and pressures among her co-workers."

barato (boROtō) the part of a gambler's winnings given to bystanders for luck

"I was lucky to receive the **barato** from the gambler who thought that such generosity would help him sustain his winning streak."

baric (BARik) pertaining to weight

"The minister told the fat woman that her concerns should be more spiritual and less **baric**.

Barmecidal (B*AW*RmuSĪD′l) providing an illusion of plenty or abundance

"Many Democrats have held that the prosperity of the 1980s was **Barmecidal**, because the government was spending too much money and spending it on the wrong things."

barnumize to advertise with outrageous or lavish claims

"When we heard the advertiser say that students would talk like William F. Buckley after only two lessons, we knew he was **barnumizing**."

"It is **Barnumism** that prompts clergymen to tell their flocks that they must fight the Confederates till Hell freezes, and then fight them on the ice."
Daily Telegraph, October 20, 1862

This word comes from P. T. Barnum (1810–1891), whose fame began in 1842 and whose "Greatest Show on Earth" (a lavish claim typical of Barnum) combined with Bailey in 1881 to form the Barnum & Bailey Circus.

barratry (BARutrē) the practice of encouraging or inciting lawsuits, often applied to lawyers who would have an interest in such suits

"Because lawsuit-happy Americans have joined **barratry**-prone lawyers, insurance and product costs have increased even beyond the general rate of inflation."

"Barratry" comes from Middle English *barratrie* ("sale of church offices"), which in turn comes from Old

French *barateour* ("swindler") and may be related to "barter."

basilect   the least prestigious dialect in a language

> "The aristocratic-looking hotel clerk regarded the Englishwoman's Cockney speech as a **basilect**."

bathos   (BĀthos)   a descent from the elevated to the commonplace in writing or speech, as when a writer aims for the sublime but hits the ridiculous

> "The slogan 'For God, for country, and for U.N.C.' illustrates **bathos** by ending with a descent in significance."

benthopelagic   (BENtho•peLAJik)   inhabiting the ocean deep

> "Only deep-sea divers ever see those **benthopelagic** fish up close."

bever   (BĒver)   a between-meal snack

> "At two o'clock she enjoyed a **bever** to stave off hunger till dinner."

"Bever" (literally, "drinking," especially of alcohol) originates from the same root as "beverage" and, in fact, "beer" and "imbibe." All those words share the Latin *bi-bo* (simply a repetition of the *bi* sound) root. From *bi-bo* came the Latin word *bibere* ("to drink"). The second "b" disappeared to form "beer" and became "v"

37

to form "bever" and "beverage," "v" and "b" being related pronunciations often interchanging in the shaping of language.

Ultimately, the Latin *bi-bo* comes from Indo-European *poi* or *pi*. Hence the English words "**po**table," "**po**tion," **po**ison" (originally simply "a special drink," the same as "potion"), and even "sym**po**sium" (originally and literally, "a coming together to drink") also originate therefrom.

bibliobibuli (BIBlēō · BIByulī)   people who read too much, oblivious of the real world

"Many of the **bibliobibuli** pride themselves on finding phallocentric imagery in literature while they have little practical understanding of the world around them."

bibliotaph (BIBlēutaf) one who hoards or hides books

"In a totalitarian society one must become a talented **bibliotaph** or else one's books may literally go up in smoke."

biduous (BIDy*uu*s)   lasting two days

"When we asked the stuffy professor how his weekend was, he replied, 'It was **biduous.**'"

bilocation (bī · l'KĀshun)   the condition of being in two places simultaneously

"Sometimes I wish I could go to parties and write at home simultaneously, though I have never been good at **bilocation**."

blithemeat (BLĪ*TH*mēt) an entertainment to celebrate the birth of a child

"The meal honoring the release of their latest book was like a **blithemeat**, for they had been 'with book' for such a long time."

blumba (BL*U*Mbu) a certifying metal tag attached to kosher meat

"The Jewish deli owner looked for the **blumba** before he accepted the meat as kosher."

blype (blīp) a piece of skin that peels off after a sunburn

"She stayed so long in the sun that she lost several **blypes**."

bodega (bōDĀgu) a small grocery store

"The **bodegas** I prefer are mom-and-pop establishments, though I have often gone into 7-Elevens."

bodkin a blunt, thick needle

"He used a **bodkin** to draw the ribbon through the casing."

Boeotian (bēŌshun) one who dislikes certain works of art or literature because he or she does not understand them

> " 'I'm not a **Boeotian**,' the senator claimed. 'I just don't like obscene art.' "

The term pertains also to people who are rude and unlettered. It originates from association with the ancient Boeotians, an agricultural and pastoral people of east central Greece. They were belittled by Athenians who considered them as dull and thick as their atmosphere.

bollards (BOl*e*rds) the posts placed in front of supermarkets to keep people from walking off with shopping carts

> "She resented the **bollards** because she wanted to take her grocery cart to her car rather than to drive her car to her grocery cart."

booby the player with the lowest score

> "Whenever we played gin rummy, he was the **booby**."

bottega (bōTĀgu) the studio of an artist or a place where students and apprentices learn

> "After school she would always go to the **bottega**, where she would learn art from the master."

brash, spate sudden rain

"Take an umbrella just in case you encounter a **brash**."

bream   to clean the bottom of a ship

"The ship's bottom had to be **breamed** to rid it of barnacles and other debris."

brevirostrate   (breviROStrāt)   having a short nose

"He was so **brevirostrate** that his nose was almost invisible."

brocage, **brokage**, **brokerage**   a pimp's wages

"The pimp enjoyed collecting his **brocage** from the prostitute."

This obsolete word comes from the word "broker." Although today brokers deal in stocks or real estate, a broker was originally a *brocheor*, one who "broke" open and sold wine from the tap (he was also called a "tapster"). Gradually, "broker" referred to any peddler or small trader, then to a dealer in secondhand goods, and by the sixteenth century, to a go-between, including a matchmaker and a "pander" (pimp, that is).

brockle   likely to break a fence, especially referring to cattle

"The **brockle** crowd needed only a little prodding to go wild and tear apart everything in sight."

41

bromatology   a treatise or essay on food

"Since he was a talented writer and a gourmet, he
felt driven to write a **bromatology.**"

bumfodder   toilet paper; also, a collection of dubious
or unnecessary documents

"Government officials love mounds of documents
that to us ordinary citizens are **bumfodder.**"

C

cachet (kaSHĀ) a prestigious or official sign of approval, as a seal, stamp, statement, or other endorsement

"The individualistic student said that he needed no **cachet** from any authority figure."

callisteia (kaliSTĪu) beauty prizes

"She was a homely woman to whom **callisteia** would never be given."

callomania (kalōMĀnēu) the delusion that one is beautiful

"Instead of suffering from **callomania**, most women suffer from the erroneous belief that they are unattractive."

calumet (KALyumet) an American Indian peace pipe

"The gangs will do well to replace their smoking guns with smoking **calumets**."

Since a pipe is a long reed, it's not surprising that "calumet" originates from a root meaning "reed." The Greek word for "small reed"—*calamellus*—has given us "caramel" (the sweet that comes from sugarcane).

camarilla   (kamuRILu)   a leader's confidential advisers

"Hillary Rodham Clinton is not only the first lady but also a significant member of the president's **camarilla**."

camouflet   (KAMuflā)   a bomb, mine, or other underground explosive device that makes a cavity but does not break the surface

"The **camouflet** left a sealed pocket of smoke and gas."

campestral   (kamPEStrul)   pertaining to level ground

"It was an expansive **campestral** site, rich in wild plants that people would never see in the city."

Canossa   (kuNAWsu)   a scene or place of humiliation and submission

"Former President Bush went to his **Canossa** when he broke his pledge of no new taxes."

cap-a-pie   (KAPupē)   from head to foot

"They were told that no one entered that crime-ridden neighborhood without being armed **cap-a-pie**."

cardiomegaly (KARdēō • MEGulē) pathological enlargement of the heart

> "His was a giving spirit, a big heart, a **cardiomegaly** of the soul."

For information about the *cardi* root, see "tachycardia."

cartnapping retail-food-industry term for the theft of shopping carts

> "The grocery store installed bollards to prevent **cartnapping**."

cathexis (kuTHEKsis) a passionate attachment to a person, idea, or emotion

> "His attachment and attraction to her reached the level of a **cathexis**."

The two main roots in this word are *cath* ("down") and *ex* ("hold"), the idea being that something is held on to, or held down, and not released. The *ex* originates from the Indo-European root for "hold": *segh*. The root appears virtually intact in "**Sieg**fried" (literally, "victory peace"; *sieg* meant "having a hold," or "conquest"— "victory," that is).

Segh produced the Greek word for "hold" (as well as for "having or being in a certain condition")—*ekhein* (the "s" having dropped out)—which in turn has given us "h**ec**tic," "ca**ch**exia," and "aprose**x**ia."

Also related to *segh* is Greek *skholē* ("a holding back,

45

stop, leisure"), which has given us "**sch**ool" and "**sch**olar." The idea is that school is where one goes, and scholarship is what one practices, when one has leisure and is not really working.

caudal   pertaining to a tail

"We were impressed by the monkey's **caudal** dexterity."

cavernicolous   (kav*er*NIKulus)   living in a cave

"The Flintstones were **cavernicolous** cartoon characters."

cedilla   (seDILu)   voiceless sound

"She explained that the mark under the letter 'c' in French was a **cedilla** to indicate that the letter is pronounced like an 's.'"

cena   last supper

"He hoped that the food was his **cena**, so bad was its taste."

chaetophorous   (kēTOF[u]rus)   in need of a shave ("bristle-bearing")

"The **chaetophorous** rock star George Michael always looks as if he has a two-day beard growth."

chaogenous   (kāOjenus)   arising out of chaos

46

"One of the **chaogenous** results of the French Revolution was the Reign of Terror."

For information about the *gen* part of this word, see "gnomon."

cholelithotomy (KŌle • lithOTumē) surgical removal of a gallstone

"He told most of his friends that he had had a **cholelithotomy**; it seemed to garner more sympathy than when he told others that he had had a gallstone removed."

chromatocracy (krōmuTOKrusē) government by a group of a particular skin color

"The black woman rightfully criticized the Founding Fathers for having excluded black people from participation in their **chromatocracy**."

chrysograph (KRISugraf) a manuscript written in ink containing gold or silver in powdered form

"The fancy invitation resembled an old ornate **chrysograph**."

chubby chaser a person who is attracted to overweight people

"The **chubby chaser** would become visibly excited around people who were pleasingly plump."

cicatrix (SIKutriks)   the scar that forms on a wound that has healed

"The prisoner had a **cicatrix**, which formed as a result of a cut he received in a fight."

cicisbeo (chēchizBĀō)   a married woman's acknowledged lover or gallant

"Since she was a woman of fame and power, everyone—even her husband—came to accept her **cicisbeo**."

cinqasept   a short visit to one's lover (literally "from five to seven P.M.")

"Somehow the congressman found time to schedule a **cinqasept** with an attractive woman."

cocarde (koKAWRD)   the emblem on the wing of a warplane that indicates which country it is from

"That the **cocardes** on the planes flying over Iraq were American was a source of great pride for many, but of great shame for others."

One might think of displaying an emblem of one's country as a cocky thing to do. For the *coc* in "cocarde" and the *coc* in "cocky" are related, both referring to the male fowl that struts his stuff. The "cockade" ("hat ornament worn as a badge," or "military emblem worn on the hat") comes from the same French word, *cocarde*. It is noteworthy, too, that a plane's cockpit got its name from its resemblance to the pit in which cockfights were held. Planes—and the people who fly them—are, all in all, quite cocky.

cockalorum   a man with delusions of grandeur

"When the bigoted man ran for the presidency, he was regarded by most people as a **cockalorum**."

coffle   (KAWful)   a line of convicts, slaves, or animals fastened together

"In *Take the Money and Run* Woody Allen plays a convict who, in one scene, is connected to other convicts in a **coffle**."

commensal   taking meals together; one individual or group benefiting from and not competing with another

"Clever dinner chat was high among their list of **commensal** pleasures."

The *mens* part of this word comes from the Latin word, *mensa*, meaning "table" (hence, the table where the meals are eaten). Note that one definition of "mensal" is "belonging to or used at the table."

commination   a threat of divine punishment

"The prophets warned disobedient sinners, using **comminations**."

compathy (KOMputhē) the sharing of feelings with others

"In this sensitivity group we encourage **compathy**."

compeer (KOMpir) one having equal rank, position, ability

"Fortunately Hitler as a strategist was not the **compeer** of Napoleon."

comprobatio the use of compliments to gain the favor of one's judges or audience

"When the defense counsel complimented the jury on their high intelligence, we knew she was using **comprobatio**."

contesseration the act of making friends

"When I handed my learned colleague the book *How to Win Friends and Influence People*, he handed it back, saying that I needed to be more concerned with ideas and less concerned with **contesseration**."

convive (KŌNvēv) a dinner guest or companion

"Because of his wit, Oscar Wilde was considered an excellent **convive**."

coparcener a person who shares equally with others in an inheritance

"At the reading of the will, the brother was disappointed to hear that he and his sister were **coparceners**."

coprolite   fossilized excrement

"The object you're holding is not an ordinary fossil; it is a **coprolite**, the fossilized dung of some animal long dead."

coruscation   (ko*r*uSKĀshun)   a brilliant flash of wit

"The brilliant conversationalist Oscar Wilde was known for his **coruscation**."

countersuggestible   tending to do the opposite of what is suggested

"Whenever I want her to do something, I suggest the opposite, exploiting her rebellious, **countersuggestible** nature."

couvade   (k*u*VOD)   a childbirth ritual among primitive people in which the father of a newborn goes through motions as if he had given birth

"Fathers can go through all the **couvade** they want to, pretending that they are giving birth, but they still will not know what it is actually like to give birth."

"Couvade" comes from Old French *couver,* meaning "to hatch or sit," as on an egg. The *cou* part comes from an Indo-European root, *keu,* meaning "to bend"; hence, "a round object" (bent all the way around). It has ultimately given us a number of English words—for example, "couvade" (in the sense of bending down; hence, lying down), "cube" and "cubicle" (from a Latin word meaning "to lie in bed," originally referred to a bedroom), "incubate" (from Latin *incubare*: "to hatch, lie down upon"), "succubus" (see entry in this dictionary), "cubit" (originally, "a bend of the elbow," then a unit of measurement from elbow to finger), "recumbent" ("lying back," "reclining"; see also "recumbentibus"), "succumb" (literally, "lying under," hence, "yielding to superior force"), and "cupola" (literally "little tub," in which one might lie).

cynophilist (siNOFulist)   a dog lover

"You might say that theirs was a mutual love: he was a **cynophilist**, and his dog was, in the literal sense, a philanderer—a lover ("phil") of man ("andro").

cynophobia (SĪNuFŌbēu)   fear of dogs

"Except for his slight anxiety around pit bulls, he has almost gotten over his **cynophobia**."

The *cyn* in "cynophilist" and "cynophobia" is, not surprisingly, related to the *can* in "canine." Both roots come from the ancient root, *kuon,* meaning "dog." "Cynosure" ("center of attention"), below, means literally "dog's tail." It is interesting to note that "cynic" literally means "doglike," which the original cynics were thought of as being. Finally, the **Can**ary Islands got their name from their indigenous wild dogs; the bird, in turn, got its name from those islands.

cynosure (SĪNush*er*) a person or thing is a center of attention

"Wherever she goes, Madonna is a **cynosure**."

D

dactylograde (dakTILugrād)   walking on one's toes

"People, who walk on the soles of their feet, are plantigrades, but cats and dogs are **dactylogrades**."

dactylonomy (daktiLONumē)   the practice of counting on one's fingers

"When you ask small children to count to ten, you can often expect them to practice **dactylonomy**."

For information about the *nom* root, see "eunomy."

definiendum (difīnēENdum)   something to be defined, as a word in a dictionary

"Your definition should be no more complex than your **definiendum**."

dehiscence (diHISun[t]s)   the bursting open of seed pods and discharging of their seeds

"When she was seventeen her chance meeting with that boy prompted her sexual **dehiscence**."

deipnosophist (dīpNOSufist) someone skilled in making dinner-table conversation

"Because he was a **deipnosophist**, he was invited to many dinners."

delaminate   to divide into thin layers

"They **delaminated** the cream cheese and put the slices on bagels."

deltiology (deltēOLʌjē) collecting picture postcards

"Whenever he traveled to a new city, he went to a souvenir shop, where he indulged his **deltiology**."

The *delti* part of this word comes from the Greek *deltion*, a small writing tablet. It is descended from the Indo-European root, *del*, meaning "cut" or "carve" and, by extension, "suffer," "pain," or "harm." In the latter sense, we now have "con**dol**ence" and "**dol**eful." In the former sense, the **del**tion was a writing tablet (into which words were cut). (See also "logodae**dal**us.")

demimonde (demēMAWND) women who have lost social position and reputation because of promiscuity

"She had engaged in one too many escapades, so that she now belonged to the **deminonde**."

dendrochronology (DENdrō-kruNOLujē) a method of determining the age of trees by studying the growth rings

"She was so adamant about not revealing her age that it would take a **dendrochronologist** to figure it out; after all, she did have a lot of wrinkles in her face."

What, you might ask, does *dendro* have to do with trees? Well, for one thing, the *dro* in *dendro* is where the word "tree" comes from (Get it? *dro* = *tro* = tree). (By the way, it is no coincidence that **tar** comes from **trees**!) Actually, the "dro" relates to an ancient form, *deru*, which meant "solid." And, after all, trees *are* solid. So too, by the way, is that which is "**true**," for the truth holds fast! Other solid things are "**dur**able" and "en**dur**ing."

diastrophism (dīAStrufiz'm) deformation of the earth's crust, forming mountains, continents, and so on

"His depressing ideas and other internal forces effected medical changes in his outward expression, much as the earth's **diastrophism** produces mountains, oceans, and other major changes in the earth's external configuration."

dichaeologia the use of excuses to defend one's failure

"Losers rarely take responsibility for their failures but instead engage in **dichaeologia**."

didactic (dīDAKtik) inclined to give unwanted instruction; also, intended mainly to instruct

"After years of teaching, he couldn't help sounding **didactic**, even to his friends."

digamy (DIGumē) marriage after the death or divorce of first spouse

"We're hoping that his **digamy** will be successful, since he doesn't want to marry for a third time."

The major roots in this word are *di* (two) and *gam* (marry). The *di* part is *not* related to dying, though the choice of *di* over *bi* was a convenient, if unintentional, pun. *Bi* also means "two," but "bigamy" means being married to two people *at the same time*.

The *gam* part pertains to marriage and also appears in "**gam**ete" (a sperm or egg, for example) and in words ending with -*ogamy*.

digitigradient (DIJitu • GRĀDēunt) walking on the toes, like cats and dogs (see also **dactylograde**)

"On controversial issues, politicians appear to be **digitigradient** creatures, tiptoeing around points of contention."

For information about the *dig* root, see "dittography."

dilling (DILin) a child born to parents who are past the age when parents commonly have children

"As the **dilling** in the family, she's much younger than all her siblings."

diplopia (diPLŌpēu) double vision

"The woman told her ophthalmologist that the only good thing about having **diplopia** is that it appears to her that she has twice as much money in her purse as she in fact has."

discalceate (diSKALsēit) to take the shoes off

"In some cultures you are expected to **discalceate** before you enter people's homes."

displume to strip of honors

"Soldiers who commit felonies ought to be **displumed** of their medals."

dittography (diTOGrufē) unintentional repetition of written letters or words

"When he wrote 'literatature' for 'literature,' we pointed out the **dittography**."

"Ditto," which means "the same as before," and which is from Italian dialect for "said," ultimately originates from the Indo-European root, *deik*, meaning "to show," or "to utter." From this root, we have "para**di**gm" ("example," "pattern"—literally, "to show side by side"), "bene**dic**tion," "male**dic**tion" ("curse"), "**dic**tion," "ju**dic**ial" (pertaining to pronouncing an opinion or judgment), "jurisdiction," "judge" (from "judicare"), "verdict," "dictate," "condition" (as in "stipulation," "agreed-upon statement"), "index" ("indicator"—hence "forefinger," for pointing), and "digit" (finger, for pointing; see also "digitigradient"). Also, from the Germanic change of the "d" to "t," we have "teach," "token" ("mark," "sign"), and perhaps even "toe" (another digit, from *taichwō*).

diurnation (dierNĀshun) the habit of sleeping during the daytime

"His new night job reversed his previous sleeping habits and required **diurnation**."

divan (dīVAN) smoking room

"Because of changing attitudes, smokers couldn't find a **divan** and so were required to abstain from smoking."

dixit an unconfirmed, sometimes dogmatic statement

"He insisted on proven statements, not **dixits**."

dogfall a fall in which both wrestlers come down together

"When the professional wrestlers collided, they treated the fans to a **dogfall**."

dysonogamia marriage between persons of markedly different ages

"The playboy had a reputation as a dirty old man long before his union—a **dysonogamia**—with a woman several decades his junior. "

For information about the *gam* root, see "digamy."

dyspnea (DIS[P]nēu) labored breathing

"**Dyspnea** was yet another consequence of his heavy smoking."

The *pn* part of "dyspnea" comes from the ancient root, *pneu*, meaning "breath," from which we ultimately get also "pneumonia." Note, the *pneu* came from *pleu*, which means, and sounds like, "flow," as in "air flow" (i.e., "breathing"). That root has also given us "pulmonary," "flying," "floating," "fowl," and "antipluvial," above.

The *dys* part of "dyspnea" means "difficult" or "labored." If we replace the *dys* with *eu*, which generally means "good," we have the word for normal respiration: "eupnea."

dysrhythmia (disRITHmēu) jet lag

"When she travels from L.A. to New York, she usually complains of **dysrhythmia**."

E

echard (eKA*W*RD) water of the soil not available to plants

"Ideas for which people are not ready are no more helpful to them than **echard** is to plants."

echolalus (ekōLĀlus) an individual who repeats what he or she hears without comprehending

"When the seven-year-old evangelist quoted Scripture he had memorized, he was accused of being an **echolalus**, repeating what he didn't understand."

eclectic pertaining to choosing the best from many possibilities

"His philosophy is **eclectic**, reflecting a wide reading of numerous schools, traditions, and theories."

effigiate (iFIJēāt) to make a statue of

"The amply **effigiated** emperor had many admirers and many detractors throughout the kingdom."

63

The *figi* in "effigiate" (in other words, "to make an effigy") comes from the Indo-European root, *dheigh*, meaning "to knead dough," or "to shape clay." From it, we get "dough," "dairy" (originally a place for kneading dough), "la**d**y" (originally the "loaf-kneader" of the household), "dig," and "ditch." And by a change that sometimes occurred from the Indo-European "d" to the Latin "f," we also ultimately get "figure" (originally, the form or shape resulting from kneading), "fiction" (fashioned, formed; hence, created, invented), "figment" (a creation of one's imagination), as well as "effigy," a sculpted or painted likeness of a person (often derogatory).

eloign, eloin   to keep at a distance

"When he has that nasty cough, we are careful to **eloign** ourselves from him so as to avoid catching his disease, whatever it might be."

"Eloign" comes from a variant of the Late Latin *ēlongāre* (from *ex*, "away," plus *longē*, "distant"). Ultimately it is related to most "long" words, such as "long," "elongate," "longitude," "prolong," and "oblong," as well as "**leng**th," "**ling**er" ("to make longer"), and "Lent" (from Old English *lengten*; refers to the lengthening of the days in the season of spring.)

elozable   (eLŌZub′l)   willing to accept flattery

"Those people are insecure, unused to any praise, and therefore highly **elozable**."

emacity   (eMAsitē)   an itch to be buying

"Merchants love materialistic, status-seeking customers for their **emacity**."

embolalia (embōLĀLyu), **embulalia** (embyuLĀLyu)
the insertion of nonsense into speech, as in schizophrenia;
hesitation forms in speech—"you know," "um," "uh," and,
like, other things we sometimes say when we aren't sure
what to say. Right? Okay?

"Anemic vocabularies and the **embulalic** 'you
know' are linguistic staples for MTV."

embower   (imBOUer)   to hide in foliage

"The **embowering** robber was behind our largest
shrub."

embracery   the attempt by bribery or other means to
influence a court

"Offering the jurors money to acquit his cousin was
clearly **embracery** and unquestionably grounds for
a mistrial."

embrocation (embruKĀshun)   lubricating or rubbing
the body

"They gave the masseuse oil for **embrocation**."

ephebic   (iFĒbik)   of a youth just entering manhood

"She recalled with fondness looking at the magazine *Tiger Beat*, in which were featured her favorite **ephebic** celebrities."

ephemeromorph (iFEM*eru*mo*rf*) biologist's term for forms of life that are so low they cannot be classified as either animal or vegetable

"The **ephemeromorph** you're talking about is considered a plant at one time of day and an animal at another."

"Most people who knew him regarded him as little more than an **ephemeromorph**, so disgustingly low and vulgar that one couldn't be sure whether he was even an animal, much less a human being."

epigone (EPug*ō*n) a descendant less gifted than his or her ancestors

"Followers of the French philosopher Descartes were mere **epigones** and couldn't come close to equaling the intelligence of their inspiration."

epinosic (epuN*Ō*Sik) **gain** secondary advantages obtained from illness, such as receiving increased attention

"I wasn't sure whether she was really sick or just seeking attention and other **epinosic gains**."

"Epinosic" contains two main roots: *epi* ("besides," "around," "in addition") and *nos* ("disease"). *Nos* comes from the Greek *nosos* ("disease") and also appears in words beginning with *noso-* (see "nosology" and "nosomania").

epiphenomenon a secondary complication during the course of an illness

> "What she is suffering from now is not, strictly speaking, part of her original illness but rather an **epiphenomenon** of it."

epiplexis (epiPLEKsis) the use of the claim that a *sensible* person must surely see the truth; the use of a question to chastise someone, as in "How could you do something so stupid?"

> "When she tactlessly assured us that 'any fool knows that,' we thought that it was perhaps she who was the fool for making such an **epiplexis**."

epistolary (uPIStulerē) presented in the form of letters

> "Saint Paul's letters constitute **epistolary** Scripture."

equipotent (ēkwuPŌtent) being equally powerful

> "The political scholar claimed that the United States and the former Soviet Union were never **equipotent** because of the latter's fundamentally unsound economy."

equiprobable (ēkwuPRObub′l)   being equally likely

"Bertrand Russell regarded the existence of God and the existence of a teacup orbiting a far-off planet as **equiprobable**."

ergasiophobia (*er*GASēōFŌbēu),   **ergophobia** (*ER*guFŌbēu)   fear of working; a surgeon's fear of operating in spite of a need to do so

"The habitually unemployed man was accused of **ergasiophobia**."

ergophile (*ER*gufīl)   one who loves work

"The **ergophile** says that he doesn't consider his job work, since he'd rather be doing it than anything else."

ergophobe (*ER*gufōb)   one who fears or hates work

"We need eager, hard workers, not lazy people, malingerers, and **ergophobes**."

eristic (iRIStik)   enjoying argument for its own sake

"Far from being **eristic**, she is reluctant to argue and will do so only if she finds a sound, logical basis."

"Eristic" comes ultimately from *Eris*, the name of the Greek goddess of discord. It was Eris who tossed a golden apple of discord to the guests at the wedding feast of Peleus and Thetis. The apple, inscribed "To the fairest," was thrown intentionally to cause mischief because Eris hadn't been invited. When three goddesses claimed it, Paris, prince of Troy, had to judge which one was fairest. When he chose Aphrodite, the other two hated him for his decision. Aphrodite later helped Paris elope with Helen to Troy, precipitating the Trojan War.

erotesis   (eruTĒsis)   a rhetorical question

   " 'Why don't you cut the **erotesis** and simply say what you mean?' he asked, ironically using a rhetorical question of his own."

eumoirous   (y*u*M*OI*rus)   being lucky or happy as a result of being good

   "Good things seemed almost always to come to the **eumoirous** young man, who cared more about virtue than exploitation."

euneirophrenia   (y*u*NĪrōFRĒnēu)   a peaceful state of mind following a pleasant dream

   "After the enjoyable dream, she basked in the resulting **euneirophrenia**."

eunomy   (Y*U*numē)   the state of being well governed

   "No nation has achieved utopia, but we are much closer to eunomy than most of the nations of Eastern Europe."

The *nomy* part of this word comes from the Indo-European root *nem*, meaning "divide, take, allot." The root has given us the English word "nomad" (a wanderer who, in a sense, is seeking an allotment, or division, of pastureland), "nemesis" (one who allots justice by seeking retribution; see also "wither**nam**"), "number" (resulting from the division, or counting, of things), "numismatics" (pertaining to coins, which are alloted, or counted), "nimble" (in essence, able to take quickly), as well as words pertaining to laws.

Greek *nomos* means "measure," "law." Laws are systematically established and laid down, and they can be "measures"—procedures, that is, for carrying out something. Thus, for example, astro**nom**y pertains to the scientific laws or principles of matter in outer space, and auto**nom**y pertains to self-government. (See also "heteronomous" and "dactylonomy.")

euphelicia (y*u*fuLIS*ē*u) good health from having all one's wishes granted

"Those who were less happy and healthy envied his **euphelicia** and were saddened by their many ungranted wishes."

eusystolism (y*u*SISToliz′m) the use of initials in place of indelicate phrases, as in "s.o.b." for "son of a bitch"

"Instead of cussing I prefer to use such **eusystolisms** as 'SNAFU,' so that I won't offend people."

eutexia (y*u*TEKsēu)   the quality of melting easily

"I asked the former chemistry professor why he was working at the ice-cream store and he said, 'I like being around that which displays **eutexia.**'"

evert (ēVE*R*T)   to turn inside out

"They experienced confusion and conflict as they came to believe that historical studies **everted** their religion."

expromission (eksprōMISHun)   responsibility for another's debts

"Because of their parents' **expromission**, the children were released from their debts."

extradictionary   consisting in deeds, not words

"The explorer boasted to the audience that his fame rested on **extradictionary**, not linguistic, actions."

extrapunitive   behaving hostilely toward other people or objects, usually to rid oneself of frustration

"They were habitually **extrapunitive**, refusing to take responsibility for their own mistakes."

exungulate (egZUNgy*u*lāt)   to trim or cut nails or hooves

"Since his fingernails were longer than his wife's, he decided that he needed to be **exungulated**."

The *ung* part of this word ultimately comes from the Indo-European root *onogh* (or *ongh* or *nogh*), meaning "nail," "claw," "hoof." Its most common contribution to English is "nail" (from Old English *naegl*), as in "fingernail" and "toenail."

eyeservice   work done only when the boss is looking

"When the boss was around, he would work with manic intensity, but he was merely paying **eyeservice** to his job."

F

factotum (fakTŌTum) a person having many and various duties to perform

"Because of his many skills and talents, he is our **factotum**."

The *tot* part of this word is, quite logically, related to the word "total," since the factotum seemingly does the total number of jobs there is. Both words descend from the Latin *totus,* meaning "swollen to capacity," "full." *Totus* originates from the Indo-European root, *teuta,* meaning "tribe"—thus, the **total** number of members of a group of people. From that root comes the name for the Germanic people (tribe) called "Teutons."

fetch light, **corpse candle** a spectral light supposedly seen before a person's death, traveling from the person's house to the grave

"The parapsychological skeptic held that the alleged **fetch light** was produced by flashlights and mirrors."

fideism   (FIdēiz′m)   a dependence on faith rather than reason

"When Martin Luther held that faith must tear out the eyes of reason, he was expressing **fideism**, toward which many Enlightenment thinkers such as Thomas Jefferson were later antagonistic."

filipendulous   (filuPENjulus)   hanging by a thread

"Like wind chimes, his fate was **filipendulous**."

fillip   to flick something with a sudden jerk of a forefinger from the thumb

"They **filliped** some crumbs off the table."

filtrate   strained liquid

"The **filtrate** had a different consistency from the original liquid."

fimetarious   (fimuTERēus),   **fimicolous**   (fiMIKulus) living in excrement

"Dung beatles are **fimetarious**."

Considering that the *fimi* part of "fimicolous" comes from a Latin word (*fimus*) for something as lowly and dull-sounding as dung, it is quite remarkable how diversely significant the root actually is. In fact, the Latin word *fimus* comes from *fumas,* meaning "smoke" ("fume" also comes from *fumas*), and it is the abstract senses of "smoke"—such as "cloud," "fragrance," even "spirit" and ultimately "mind"—that give *fim* its surprisingly lofty heritage.

The Indo-European, and thus the ultimate, root of *fimus* is *dheu,* meaning "to smoke, dust." From it we have "dust," "dusk," "dove" (a dark-colored bird), "deaf" (clouded senses; from Germanic *daubaz*), "dumb" (clouded senses), "dull" (not sharp, especially in the senses), "doldrums," "dizzy" (from Old English *dysiz,* meaning "foolish"), and even "deer" (derived from the breath of the animal, which is visible on cold days; from Germanic *diuzam* meaning "breathing creature").

Further, the change from Indo-European "d" to Greek "t" and "th" has generated "typhoid" and "typhus" (from Greek *typhois* meaning "fever, delusion") and words ending in *-thymia* (from Greek *thumos,* meaning "soul," or "spirit"), which designate, for example, medical conditions of the mind or will.

Still further, the change from Indo-European "d" to Latin "f" has generated "fume," "perfume," "obfuscate," and so on.

flitwite   a fine for fighting

"The teachers wanted to punish their pupils for fighting not with a stick or verbal abuse but with a reasonable **flitwite**."

The *wite* part of this word is still used by itself in English (borrowed from Scottish) to mean "blame," "fault" (see also "lairwite"). Old English *wīte,* which meant "fine, penalty," is ultimately derived from Indo-European *weid,* meaning "to see." It is, therefore, related in origin to a number of words that pertain to seeing, overseeing (including uncovering blame and administering fines), guiding, and learning—for example, "guide" (remember, "gu," "gw," and "w" are closely related), "vision" (from Latin *vidēre,* meaning "to see, look"; remember that "v" and "w" are closely related, and "w" is pronounced "v" in some languages), "idea" (the "w" having been dropped entirely—literally, "appearance"), and "Hades" ("the underworld"—that which is not seen). In addition, we have "wise," "wisdom," "wit," and even "history" (from Indo-European *widtor* and then Greek *histor,* meaning "wise," or "learned"; see also "polyhistorian").

floccillation (floksuLĀshun) searching for imaginary objects; picking at the bedclothes by a delirious patient

> "The doctor explained that some people pick at bedclothes because they itch, but others engage in **floccillation** because of high fever or exhaustion."

florescence a successful or prosperous period

> "After years of practice and hard work, he enjoyed the **florescence** of his skills."

floromacy the belief that flowers have feelings and will respond to kindness as well as cruelty

> "Since he never talked to the flower, he probably didn't believe in **floromancy.**"

fortnight   two weeks

"He received a paycheck every **fortnight**."

frass   insect excrement

"I know we have insects because I saw some **frass** on the floor."

"I wouldn't say you're talking BS; let's just say it's a bit of **frass**."

fugleman   (FYUG′lmun)   one who sets an example

"We need a **fugleman** who will inspire people by his example."

A "fugleman" once meant "a model soldier." In German, *Flugelmann* means "soldier" (but literally "man on the wing"; in military usage, "wing" is an army's left or right flank). *Flugel*, meaning "wing," originates from the same Indo-European root that gives us "fowl": *pleu*. "Fowl" comes from the Middle English *foul* and Old English *fugol*. The Indo-European "p" in "pleu" had become Germanic "f" to produce *flug*; then by a process in which letter positions are inverted (called "metathesis"), *flug* had become *fugl* (*fugol*). (For more information about *pleu*-root descendants, see "antipluvial.")

fumacious   (fyuMĀshus)   addicted to smoking

"The smoker accepted the idea that she was **fumacious** and used that as an excuse not to exercise enough willpower to stop."

funicular   (fy*u*NIKyulur)   worked by or hanging from a rope or cable

"The flagpole contained a **funicular** mechanism."

furfuration   (f*er*f[y]uRĀshun)   the scaling off of dead skin in small particles, such as dandruff

"When they used the anti-dandruff shampoo, they no longer had to worry about **furfuration**."

G

galanty (guLANtē), **mackninny** a puppet show

"Children usually like a **galanty**, especially if the puppets look silly."

"The cult followers were part of a massive **galanty**, and their leader was the puppet master."

gargalesthesia the sensation caused by tickling

"**Gargalesthesia** can be pleasant, provided that it is brief and it is caused by a tickler you don't dislike."

Presumably, the *gargal* part of this word is directly related to the root of "gargle." After all, "gargle" comes from an Old French word (*gargouiller*) meaning "throat," and when we gargle we are, in a sense, tickling the throat. "Gargle" ultimately comes from the Indo-European root *gwere*, or *garg*, meaning "swallow," or "throat sounds." Merely by saying that root, one can gather that its origin is onomatopoeic, since it really does sound similar to gargling.

From that root, we now have also "**vor**acious" (pertaining to swallowing up; *gwer* became *wer*, which became *vor*—remember, "v" and "w" are closely related), "de**vour**," "-**vor**ous" words (such as "carnivorous"— "meat-eating"), "re**gurg**itate," "**garg**oyle" (a grotesquely shaped rain spout; from Latin *gargulio*, meaning "windpipe"), and so on.

gelastic   (juLAStik)   pertaining to laughter

   "After the bad news, he was not in a **gelastic** mood."

gelogenic   (jelōGENik)   tending to produce laughter

   "We weren't sure which was more **gelogenic**, the comedian's joke or his unintentional fart."

   For information about the *gen* part of this word, see "gnomon."

geloscopy   (jelOSkupē)   a technique for determining people's character by observing their laughter

   "I disagree in principle with **geloscopy**, since people reveal their character not in their laughter but in their actions."

genetic fallacy   an argument that something is invalid because of its origin or historical background, as in dismissing a scientist's latest claim because that scientist's first major publicized claim was proved false

"To argue that astronomy is unscientific because it evolved from astrology is to commit the **genetic fallacy**."

For information about the *gen* part of this word, see "gnomon."

geophagia (gēoFĀj[ē]u), **pica** (PĪku) an abnormal desire to eat something not usually regarded as food—for example, soil or chalk—sometimes exhibited during pregnancy or hysteria.

"We think that her **geophagia** was due to a mineral deficiency, since that is a common reason for young children to eat dirt."

"The tabloid's editors have a **pica** to eat up whatever trash they can get their insensitive, dirty hands on."

Phagia- and *-phagous* are Greek-derived suffixes pertaining to eating—for example, "sarcophagus," literally, "flesh-eaten." The *phag* part comes from the Indo-European root, *bhag*, meaning "share (particularly food)" (the Indo-European "b" sometimes becomes Greek "p"). In Sanskrit, *Bhaga* is the god of wealth, literally "Distributor"—hence the *Bhagavad-Gita* is Hinduism's "song of the lord." Also, "**pag**oda" (from Sanskrit *bhagavatī*) was originally the word for "holy temple." See also "onychophagy" and "tachyphagia."

glebe church land

"The church rented out its **glebe** and made a good sum of money."

gnomon   (NŌmon)   the pin or plate of a sundial that throws its shadow on the face of the dial

"My sundial needs a shadow; do you have an extra **gnomon** I can borrow?"

The *gn* part of this word is the basis of a prolific Indo-European root: *gn* or *gen*, meaning "to know" and, in the sense of "conceiving," "to beget." The word "know" itself contains the *gn* root (German "g" changed to "k" in English, the two letters normally having related sounds). To **kin**dle a flame is to beget the flame ("**ign**ite" is its Latin cognate). So too we have "**kin**" and even "**can**" ("know how").

Other "gn" words include "generate," "genitals," "generic," "genesis," "genus," "pregnant" ("before birth"), "miscegenation," "gentle" (orginally "born in the family"—hence "well bred"), "gentry," "ingenious" (having inborn talent), "engine" (a product of inborn talent), "benign" (not likely to produce), "cognition," "prognosis," "diagnosis," "agnostic," "ignorance," and so on. "Gnomon," a device that makes known the time, comes from the Greek "gnomos," meaning "interpreter."

Still other words ultimately dropped the "g" (or "k"), as in "noble" (worthy of being known) and "narrative" (known—hence, "told").

For other examples of the *gn/gen* root, see also "ad ignorantiam," "agnogenic," "chaogenous," "gelogenic," "genetic fallacy," "ignivomous," "kedogenous," "philoprogenitive," "physiognomy," "stereognosis," and "unigeniture."

gomphiasis (gomFĪusis)   looseness of the teeth

"She was worried that her **gomphiasis** might cause several of her teeth to fall out."

"The new bill suffers from severe **gomphiasis**, since it makes illegal something that cannot possibly be enforced, and so lacks sturdy teeth."

grike   a narrow opening in a wooden or stone fence that allows people but not farm animals to get through

"He carefully climbed through the **grike** in the white picket fence."

grimpen   a part of a mountain that is very treacherous to climb

"If you're just beginning to learn to climb mountains, don't start out on a **grimpen**."

grisaille (griZĪ)   painting using shades of gray only, often in imitation of bas-relief

"His personality was as colorful as a **grisaille**."

groaking   staring at someone who is eating, in the hope that he'll give you something

"As we were eating, we noticed a hungry-looking man **groaking** at us."

guddle   to catch fish with the hands

"Since we didn't have a fishing rod, we tried to **guddle** some fish."

guttate   (*GU*tāt)   spotted or speckled as if by drops

"We soon realized that the rabbit's **guttate** appearance was due to a leech infestation."

The root *gutta* means "drop" and appears also in "gutter" (where drops flow), "gout" (metabolic disease once thought to be caused by drops of diseased humors), and "goiter" (from Latin *guttur*, meaning "throat," via French; enlargement of thyroid gland, which is in the throat, where water drips into the body)

guttatim   (gu*TĀ*tum)   drop by drop

"I want you to clean up the milk **guttatim**."

gynarchy   (JIn*awrkē* / GĪn*awrkē*)   rule by women

"Women aren't demanding a **gynarchy**, just more representation."

H

hamble   (AM[b]ul)   to cut off the balls of a dog's feet so he cannot hunt

"Since they didn't want the dog to hunt, they **hambled** him, making it more difficult for the dog to walk."

hamesucken   (HĀMsukun)   the assaulting of someone in his or her own house

"The police officer held that nowadays the incidence of **hamesucken** has gone up so that many people are unsafe even in their own homes."

Hame is equivalent to "home." *Sucken* is related to "seeking out," or "searching," hence "attacking." In a similar sense, "to ransack" is "to search carefully," hence "steal," or "pillage."

hammocking   putting a new television show between two established hits

"The network executives use **hammocking** to encourage people to watch new shows."

handsel (HAN[T]sul) a gift given as a token of good luck, usually at the beginning of a new enterprise

"When she opened her new business, her first customer gave her an old silver dollar as a **handsel**."

hawk to clear the throat

"Whenever he had a frog in his throat, he would begin to **hawk**."

hebdomadal (hebDOMud'l) happening every seven days

"We go to church on a **hebdomadal** basis."

hedon a unit of pleasure

"Although dark chocolate ordinarily contains more calories than milk chocolate, it gives me more **hedons**."

heft to test or gauge the weight of something by lifting

"**Hefting** a stone can be dangerous, since you may not have a good idea of its weight before you pick it up."

heteronomous (heduROnimus) subject to other's rules

"Thomas Paine was a profoundly individualistic writer who rejected **heteronomous** practices and institutions, as when he condemned Bible-based religion and questioned the authority of British colonizers."

For information about the *nom* part of this word, see "eunomy."

heuristics (hyuRIStiks) teaching or learning through discovery and investigation

"**Heuristics** is an important means of stimulating research and discovery."

hibernaculum (hīberNAKyulum), **hibernacle** (HĪber • nak′l) winter quarters

"He has a different residence for the summer; this place is his **hibernaculum**."

hiccup opening a movie with a dramatic scene and then bringing on the title and credits

"The movie began with a **hiccup**, which, since it came before the credits, he mistook for a preview to another movie."

"Hiccup" is most likely imitative of the sound of a hiccup (hence, it's onomatopoeic). The word goes back at least to the sixteenth century, when its spellings included "hyckok," "hicket," and "hickop." In 1626, the alternate spelling, "hiccough," was first used by Francis Bacon, who made a mistaken association with the word "cough"—though there was no change in the pronunciation, "HIKup."

hierofastidia (HĪerō • faSTIDēu) dislike of holy things

"Because of his **hierofastidia**, the atheist was visibly uncomfortable in the church."

holophrasis (huLAWfrusis), **holophrase** (HOLufrāz), **holophrasm** (HOLufraz′m) a whole phrase or idea expressed in one word, such as "Thanks," "More," or "Ouch!"

"His **holophrasis** was simply 'Stop!' "

holotype (HOlutip) an animal or plant selected as representative of a new species

"He was unique in so many respects that you could have sworn he was a **holotype** for a one-of-a-kind human being."

holus-bolus (HOlus • BOlus) all at one time

"He said that he wanted to complete the project **holus-bolus** rather than doing it in stages over a period of months."

homeopathy (hōmēOPuthē) therapy using doses of medicine that produce symptoms of the disease treated

"Passion flower is an ingredient in a proven **homeopathy** for nervous tension and insomnia."

homilophobia (homiluFŌbēu) fear of sermons

"The hypersensitive parishioner developed **homilophobia** and couldn't sit through a sermon without breaking out in a cold sweat."

homo unius libri (HŌmō *u*NĒus LIBrē) one whose knowledge of a subject is gained from only one book or one point of view

"The **homo unius libri** continued to insist that his was the only correct point of view and that his single source was the only source one needed to consult."

horaphthia (*hor*AFthēu) an abnormal preoccupation with one's youth

"His toupee, his hip talk, and his taste in contemporary music all reflected the seventy-year-old man's **horaphthia**."

You could probably guess that the *hor* in this word is related to "hour"—in other words, "the passage of time." "**Hor**oscope" and "**year**" are also related. *Hor* comes from the ancient root, *eir,* meaning "that which goes" (time, of course, goes like nothing else!). That root, in turn, comes from the basic root, *ei* or *i*, meaning simply "go." The *i* root has given us such words as "**i**on," "**ich**nology" ("study of footprints"), "amb**it**," "**it**inerary," "ex**it**," and even "err" (one who goes may also go astray).

hypocorism (hīPOkuriz′m)   adult imitation of baby talk; the use of nicknames

> "When I hear adults saying 'goo-goo' and 'gah-gah' and other such examples of **hypocorism**, I wonder whether *they* are the babies."

The *cor* part of this word comes from the Indo-European root, *ker*, meaning "to grow." The root has given us "cereal" (literally, "of grain"), "create," "concrete" ("to grow together"), "increase," and "recruit" ("to grow again; to raise an army"). The root is also the source of the Greek words for "boy" and "girl" (*koros* and *korē*; boys and girls grow, of course), which are the ultimate source of *korizesthai*, meaning "caress" (that which one often does with children). "Hypocorism" (literally, "to call by endearing names") comes from the Greek *hupokorizesthai*, meaning "to caress secretly." (See also "ac**cr**escent.")

hypocrisis   mockery by exaggerating an opponent's mannerisms or speech habits

> "Impressionist comedians rely on **hypocrisis** because exaggerations of people's mannerisms can be funny and memorable."

hypophora (hīPOforu)   the posing of questions to oneself and the answering of them, or a reasoning aloud

"I enjoy practicing **hypophora** because when I answer my own questions, I never have to disagree with any of the answers."

hypoprosexia (hīpō•pruSEKsēu) inability to concentrate for more than short periods

"Students with **hypoprosexia** need to train their minds to concentrate even on things that aren't immediately exciting."

I

ideomania (idēōMĀnēu)   obsession with an idea

"Their **ideomania** was so strong that they did not
want to do anything that didn't relate to their ideas."

The *man* part of this word comes from the Indo-
European root, *men,* meaning "to think" or pertaining to
conditions of the mind. To the English language, it has
given "**mnemon**ic," "mind," "mental," "reminisce,"
"mantra," "amnesia," "amnesty" ("forgotten," hence
"forgiven"), "remember," "memory," "comment" (in-
spired by thought), "admonish" (to remind strongly,
warn), "monitor" (literally, "one who reminds, warns, or
oversees"), "museum" (from *muse*—in Greek myth, a
goddess who presided over learning and arts; related to
Greek *mnasthai,* "to remember"), "music" (also from
muse), "**mon**ument" (a memorial), "summon" (related to
word meaning "to remind secretly": Latin *sub + monere;*
hence a summons is a reminder to attend court), demon-
strate (originally the appearance of an omen that reminds
or warns; later, simply to show), and "mathematics" (see
"opsimath"), as well as "maniac" and "mania." See also
"nepimnemic" and "pseudomnesia."

For information about the *ideo* part of this word, see "flitwite."

idiolalia (idēōLĀlēu) private language, sometimes invented by those of low mentality

"The bigoted preacher might as well have been speaking some **idiolalia**, his words being so non-sensically put together as to be understood only by those of the least intellect and greatest gullibility."

idiopathic (idēuPATHik) pertaining to a disease whose cause is unknown

"Instead of telling her patient that she didn't know the exact cause of the illness, she described the illness as '**idiopathic**.'"

idols of the cave errors arising from personal bias or prejudice

"When he says that Andy Warhol is the best painter of the twentieth century, he is surely just expressing one of the **idols of the cave**."

idols of the theater errors caused by perpetuation of traditional beliefs

"Her uncritical acceptance of her church's traditional doctrines will suggest to many secular people that she has fallen victim to **idols of the theater**."

ignivomous (igNIVumus)   fire-vomiting like a dragon

"He assured the children that only dragons are **ignivomous** and that dragons are legendary."

For information about the *gn* part of this word, see "gnomon."

immerge   to disappear, like the sun below the horizon or in an eclipse

"The sun **immerged** as it sank below the horizon, and another day had passed."

imperdible (imP*ER*dib'l)   incapable of being lost

"Don't lose this key; it's not **imperdible**."

In 1661, Owen Felltham used this word to describe wisdom and knowledge—and in the process gave us a little wisdom of his own: "As they [wisdom and knowledge] are harder in their acquisition, so are they more **imperdible** and steady in their stay."

Although "imperdible" is now considered obsolete and rare in English, the word remains in use in Spanish, as both an adverb and a noun. As a noun it is, quite appropriately, the word for "safety pin."

"Imperdible" is from the same root as "perdition." Indeed, perdition can be thought of as representing virtually the opposite of that which is imperdible, for "perdition" can mean "the loss of one's soul or one's ultimate happiness," "utter damnation," or "the place of eternal damnation." No matter how you look at it, perdition represents complete loss!

indehiscent (indiHIS′nt)   not opening at maturity

"Botanically, buckwheat, unlike the iris, is **indehiscent**, since it doesn't open at maturity."

inenubilable (in • en*yoo*BILub′l)   incapable of being made clear

"As long as people wear the blinders of bigotry, racial equality is an **inenubilable** concept and an unreachable dream."

infarct (INf*a*wrkt)   an area of dead tissue

"Had the local circulation not been obstructed, there would have been no **infarct** in his heart."

"Slums are a country's **infarct**."

infucation (infy*u*KĀshun)   the act of putting on makeup

"I need my lipstick, rouge, and other **infucation** supplies."

interlucation (int*er* • l*u*KĀshun)   the thinning out of trees to let in some light

"The lumberjack recommended **interlucation** to the homeowner who said that his house was too heavily shaded."

internecion (in*ter*NESHun)   mutual destruction

"We need to get rid of nuclear weapons from both sides, lest we suffer from **internecion**."

interpellation (in*ter*puLĀshun)   a formal demand that a government official's act or policy be explained

"In some European legislatures, a minister's policies or actions can be formally questioned through **interpellation**."

introjection   throwing oneself into one's work

"They were workaholics whose **introjection** at times alienated their families."

invigilate (inVIJulāt)   to supervise students at an examination

"Since I'll be carefully **invigilating** this exam, cheating may be hazardous to your grade."

irenic (īRENik)   promoting peace

"Because of all those conflicts, we need at least some **irenic** gestures."

irredenta (iriDENtu)   a region related ethnically to one nation but governed by another

"The inequities in the treaty created needless **irre-dentas** and spawned more ethnic rivalries."

isauxesis (isawgZĒsis) in an organism, the growth of a part at the same rate as the whole

"The anatomy student asked whether the growth of a baby's head in relation to the growth of the rest of its body was a case of **isauxesis**."

isochromatic (īsō · krōMATik) having the same color

" 'We need a polychromatic not an **isochromatic** Congress,' asserted the proponent of racial equality."

The *chrom* part of this word comes from the ancient root *gher*, meaning "scratch," "scrape," or "rub" and "rough surface." The Greek word *khriein* is the root of "Christ" ("the anointed") and "christen"—a rubbing, or smearing, of holy water. Even the word "cream" ultimately originates from the *gher* root.

The Greek word for color, *khroma*, arose gradually from the original *gher* root, first referring to a rough surface, then to skin, then to skin color, and finally simply to color.

isochronal (īSOKrun'l) occupying or happening in an equal amount of time

"Ironically, walking a mile and driving a mile during rush hour may be **isochronal**."

J

jehu (JĒh*u*) one who loves driving, especially fast driving

"The traffic officer said that he had little respect for **jehus**, who make the road dangerous for everyone."

jeofail (JĒfāl) a lawyer's mistake and his or her acknowledgment of it to the court

"When the lawyer mentioned again what had been stricken from the court records, her **jeofail** made some people wonder whether she was deliberately trying to manipulate the jury."

jerque (j*er*k) to search for smuggled goods

"The customs inspector began to **jerque** our luggage."

jettison to throw overboard

"Our boat will sink unless we **jettison** the equipment we don't need."

The *je* part of this word comes from the Indo-European root, *ie*, meaning "send," "throw"—especially, "throw down." It has given English such words as "jactation" (boasting; literally, "a throwing or tossing of the body"), "jest," "jet," "jetsam" (goods thrown overboard to lighten a ship's load), "jetty" (for example, a projection intentionally placed out into the sea), "gist" (the fundamental point, thrown down, as it were), "adjacent" ("lying near"—in a sense, thrown near), "abject" (literally "thrown out, cast off," hence, in a low state), "deject," "eject," "object," "reject," "trajectory," and so on.

joom to burn a forest, cultivate the land, and then abandon it

"We must no longer **joom** forests but always replant what we remove."

jornada (h*or*NOdu) a day's travel with no stops

"After our **jornada** we needed a rest from our travels."

jugulate to check or suppress by extreme measures, as, literally, by cutting the throat (jugular)

"The dictator said that those insurrectionists must be **jugulated** before they get out of hand."

K

kalon (kuLON) the ideal of physical and moral beauty

"In ancient Greece if people achieved **kalon**, they were beautiful in both body and character."

kalopsia (kaLOPsēu) condition where things appear more beautiful than they really are

"People in love have optimistic distortions in perception so that they often experience **kalopsia**."

kedogenous (keDOjunus) produced by worry

"Since most of his physical problems are **kedogenous**, he needs to learn how to manage stress."

For information about the *gen* part of this word, see "gnomon."

keraunophobia (kuRAWNōFŌbēu) fear of thunder and lightning

"His **keraunophobia** was so severe that he crawled under the bed during thunderstorms."

kerdomeletia   (kerdō • meLĒSHu), **plutomania** (plutuMĀnēu)   preoccupation with material wealth

"In the 1980s many Americans, driven by **kerdomeletia**, used unethical methods in attempting to amass wealth."

kermes   (KERmēz / kerMES)   dried insect bodies

"When asked about the texture of the pastry baklava, the entomologist likened its texture to that of **kermes**."

This word has remained nearly intact in both meaning and spelling since its Indo-European origins: *kurmi*, meaning "worm"—especially "from a worm." It has given us "worm" ("ku," "kw," and "w" are related), "**crim**son" (related to word meaning "red of the kermes"), and "**carm**ine" ("red lake," from Arabic *gimiz* [kermes] and Latin *minium* [red lead]).

kindergraph   a photograph of a child

"Grandparents love to show **kindergraphs** of their grandchildren."

kinephantom   the illusion of reverse movement in a fast-moving object, such as the spokes of a wheel

"Like a **kinephantom**, I might appear to be moving backward, though I am making slow but certain progress."

kinetosis (kinuTŌsis)   motion sickness

"Merely getting up in the morning gives me **kinetosis**."

kitchenstuff   fat and grease drippings saved for later use

"He likes using bacon grease and other **kitchenstuff** for flavoring."

L

laaba (LObu)   a storage platform beyond the reach of animals

"On the **laaba** the food was safe from the dogs and other animals."

lacuna (luK[Y]*U*nu)   a gap in evidence or data occurring in memory or consciousness

"There is a curious **lacuna** in his recollection of the events."

lairwite (LERwīt)   a fine given a married woman who has committed adultery

"The woman who was found guilty of adultery was relieved that she only had to pay a **lairwite** rather than go to prison."

Lair would seem an appropriate sound in such a word, since the offense here does concern itself with . . . well . . . with laying—lying, that is—in the wrong bed. In fact, "lair" itself is a Scottish borrowing that means "burial lot in a graveyard." In British dialect, it is a word for various resting places. The word is related to "lay," "lie," "lager" (beer laid aside to ferment), and "law," which is "laid down."

The *wite* part of "lairwite" is found also in "flitwite," another Scottish borrowing (see "flitwite").

lapidate   to throw stones, as in executing people

"In ancient times many of those guilty of capital offenses would be **lapidated**."

lassipedes   (laSIPidēz)   tired feet

"After walking all day I soaked my **lassipedes**."

lasslorn   forsaken by one's sweetheart

"The **lasslorn** groom stood, alone, at the altar wondering whether he would ever again see his bride."

latah   (LAtu)   a neurotic compulsion to imitate others in speech and action

"The religious man regretted that many other religious people are stricken with a kind of **latah**, their religion being one simply of compulsive imitation rather than one that is deeply personal, requiring people to think for themselves."

lection   reading of Scripture

"**Lection** and sermons were nearly always components in our church services."

leeward (LĒwurd [but pronounced "L*U*u(r)d" in nautical usage])   the side sheltered from the wind

"We preferred the **leeward** side of the house, since it was quieter than the windward side."

lentic   relating to or dwelling in still water

"The speaker exhorted us not to be like **lentic** fish but to dive deep into the ocean of life."

lethologica (lethōLOjiku)   the temporary inability to recall a word or a name

"Even people with good memories can experience **lethologica** until such time as they receive something to remind them of the exact word they're trying to recall."

lethonomia (lethōNŌmēu)   a   tendency   to   forget names

"I'll show you some memory aids to help you recall names so that you won't be embarrassed by **lethonomia**."

levant (liVANT)   a bet made with intent not to pay if lost; to flee one's debtors

"His previous **levant** indicated that he was one
bettor who could not be trusted."

lexicomane   a lover of dictionaries

"A true **lexicomane**, she collects dictionaries and
habitually reads them."

libation   (līBĀshun)   liquid poured ceremonially, as
in honor of a deity

"In their worship of Bacchus, wine was their **libation**."

The *lib* part of this word comes directly from the
ancient Indo-European root, *leib*, meaning "pour." From
it we now have also "littoral" (pertaining to the seashore,
where water pours in), "Lithuania" ("shoreland"), and
"libeccio" (Italian, "the south wind," which brings rain
from the Mediterranean).

liberticidal   (liB*ER*Tu • sīd'l)   destroying liberty

"The lawyer claimed that enforcement of the drug
laws has eroded the Fourth Amendment and has
been generally **liberticidal**."

logodaedalus   (lōgōDEDulus), **logodaedaly**
(loguDĒdulē)   one who is cunning in the use of words;
the ability to coin new words

"Always verbally adroit, Buckley is quite the **logodaedalus**."

Daedalus in Greek legend was known for his skill, though not with words. It was Daedalus who, for example, invented wings to escape from King Minos and flew off with his son Icarus, who was killed in flight. It was also Daedalus who, when posed with the problem of threading a spiral shell, cleverly attached a thread to an ant, which pulled the thread through the shell. (See also "**del**tiology.")

logofascinated   fascinated by words

"I'm told that the authors Berent and Evans are **logofascinated**."

logogogue   (LAWgugawg)   person who lays down the law concerning words and their use

"She claimed that she wasn't some tyrannical **logogogue** but simply one who aspired to careful usage."

logomachy   (lōGOMukē)   a dispute about words and their meanings; a quibbling over semantics that gets away from the subject; a war of words

"Having no significant disagreement about how I arrived at my claims, his criticisms were nothing more than a simplistic **logomachy**."

For information about the *machy* root, see "sciamachy."

logomisia   (lōgōMISēu)   disgust for certain words

"My **logomisia** is restricted to bigoted and other crude words, which I always avoid using and condemn."

The *mis* part of this words comes from the Indo-European root, *mei*, meaning "small." It has given us, for example, "minimum," "minute" (small amount, especially of time), "mini-" words, "minuscule," "diminish," "minor," "minister" (originally, a "minor officer" compared with the magistrate, the "major" official), and perhaps "mime" (which makes reality small), "pantomime," and "mimic."

Further, in an extended sense, that which is small may be that which is belittled, unimportant, and even bad or hated. Hence, a **mis**take or **mis**behaving is considered bad, and **mis**anthropy, **mis**ogyny, and **mis**ology are hatreds (of man, woman, and reason, respectively).

See also entries beginning with *mis-*.

M

macarism (MAKuriz′m)   the practice of making others happy by praising them

"When the author Dale Carnegie told them to lavish praise on others to make them happier, we knew that he was a proponent of **macarism**."

machicolation (muchikuLĀshun)   an opening in the floor of a gallery or chamber over an entry or passage in a castle or stronghold designed for dropping stones or boiling liquid on attackers

"Attacking forces under the **machicolation** of the castle would be greeted with a shower of heavy stones."

macrophobia   fear of long waits

"Anyone with **macrophobia** should, whenever possible, avoid going to extremely busy doctors."

mactation   the action or process of killing a sacrificial victim

"Our **mactations** have gone from human sacrifice to animal sacrifice and now drug sacrifice, drugs being society's latest scapegoat."

mahoitre   padding to make the shoulders appear larger

"I was told that former President Reagan wore a **mahoitre** or some other pad to make his shoulders appear larger, but I'm sure that he always had a good build."

maieutic   (māYUdik)   of the Socratic method of questioning to elicit and clarify others' ideas

"Borrowing from Socrates, many law professors use a **maieutic** technique to test their students' knowledge by asking a series of questions."

The term is from the Greek *maieutikos*, literally, "of midwifery," from *maia*, "midwife." Socrates, whose mother was reputed to be a midwife, was considered an intellectual midwife, because he helped his interlocutors give birth to their ideas from their pregnant minds. Socrates would elicit the ideas by asking a series of questions.

meconium   (miKŌnēum)   the excrement in the fetal intestinal tract that is discharged at birth

"The food we ate in the army would have tasted like **meconium** had it been a little fresher."

medela   apology for another's behavior or faults

"It is *he* who needs to apologize; we accept no **medela** here."

medius (MĒdēus)   the middle finger

"He showed his disrespect by raising his **medius** while lowering his other fingers."

meed   a well-deserved reward

"He accepted their **meed** for saving their dog."

melolagnia (melōLAGnēu)   sexual desire aroused by music

"They were transported by Madonna's music, which produced in them a powerful **melolagnia**."

melomaniac (melōMĀnēak)   a music lover

"A certifiable **melomaniac**, he had over a thousand CDs."

memoriter (miMORut*er*)   from memory; by heart

"She knew many biblical verses **memoriter**."

menstruum (MENZtr[*u*]um)   a month's term of office; also, a month's provisions

"At the rate at which congresspersons begin working on becoming reelected once they get into office, you would think theirs was a **menstruum** rather than a full two-year term."

mentimutation (menti•my*u*TĀshun) a change of mind

"I'm not being inconsistent; I'm simply exercising my right to **mentimutation**."

mephitis (miFĪtis) a foul odor from the earth

"The smell was so bad that, compared to it, **mephitis** would smell like the finest perfume."

mésalliance (MĀzalyonz), **misalliance** marriage with a person of inferior social status

"Even though the prince accepted a **mésalliance** instead of a marriage with royalty, he deeply loved his wife, despite her lower social status."

microtome a cutting instrument that slices thin pieces of tissue for viewing under a microscope

"When the drunken surgeon tried to use the **microtome** for slicing cheese, he was formally censured by the medical board."

mileway (MĪLwā) the time it takes to walk a mile

"His walk to the store took about nine or ten minutes, or a **mileway**."

militaster   an insignificant military man

"When the general called the arrogant private a **militaster**, he wounded the private's ego."

miniate (MINēāt), **rubricate** (R*U*brucāt)   to paint with red letters

"He suggested that we avoid using yellow paint for the letters but suggested that we **miniate** the letters."

minimifidian (minimiFIDēun)   pertaining to a minimal amount of faith

"The minister admonished her congregants, 'Your **minimifidian** attitude will get you nowhere; you must have unswerving faith if you are to enter the kingdom of heaven.'"

minimus (MINimus)   the smallest or least important person; the little finger or toe

"Each graduate instructor is a **minimus** among college teachers, since adjunct assistant professors, associate professors, and full professors all have higher standing."

miryachit (mērYOchēt)   an abnormal mimicking of everything said or done by another

"He lost all sense of self, as his **miryachit** consumed him and turned him into an imitation of everyone but himself."

misogamy (miSOGumē)   hatred of marriage

"Feminists who argue that the traditional marriage has resulted in the oppression of women have been accused of **misogamy**."

misogynist (miSOJunist)   one who hates women

"Because the philosopher Schopenhauer claimed that women have smaller brains than men, he was labeled a **misogynist**."

misology (miSOLujē)   hatred of reason

"Many learned thinkers throughout history have, in effect, equated religious orthodoxy with **misology**."

misoneist (misuNĒist)   one who hates anything new

"She's not a **misoneist**; she simply wants new ideas and new products tested before she approves of them."

misotramontanism (mīsō • truMONtuniz′m)   a hatred of the unknown

"Although it may be true that familiarity breeds contempt, the opposite is also true, since **misotramontanism** is a common repsonse to things unfamiliar."

mithridate, treacle   antidote to poison

"He eats food as though he thinks it's a **mithridate**, hoping that the more unnutritious junk he eats, the less serious will be its negative effects."

The word "mithridate" comes from Mithridates VI, King of Pontus and Bithynia, who lived from about 132 to 63 B.C. Called "the Great," he had great military ability and was one of the most formidable opponents Rome ever had. He supposedly immunized himself from poisons by constantly using antidotes, at least one of which was said to contain forty-six or more ingredients.

mithridatism   immunity to a poison effected by taking gradually increased doses of it

"Parents need to understand that they are applying the principle of **mithridatism** to their children's television watching; for, just as taking gradually increased doses of a poison supposedly makes one immune to the poison, so as children watch more and more violence on TV each day, they will soon be completely unmoved by and careless about any violence, real or make-believe, that they witness."

mizzle, scud   a fine mist of rain

"Although I enjoy feeling a mist of rain on my face, some people complain that **mizzle** is harder to deflect with umbrellas and windshield wipers than a downpour."

monism   the view that there exists only one sort of thing, such as mind or matter; the view that reality is an organic whole without independent parts.

"Spinoza adopted a **monism** in which there is really only one ultimate substance, which he called God."

monoglot   a person knowing only one language

"**Monoglots** are much more common in the United States than in Europe, where knowing two or more languages is often a necessity."

monology   (muNOLujē)   the habit of talking to oneself

"There's nothing unusual or abnormal about **monology**, provided that you don't disagree with yourself."

monticule   a small mountain

"The articulate little boy explained that he couldn't go out to play because he was 'buried in a **monticule** of homework.' "

"The structure called Mount Trashmore in Virginia Beach isn't really a mountain, but an artificially created **monticule**, composed primarily of the city's garbage and used as a city park."

morganatic   pertaining to marriage between social unequals in which titles and estates aren't passed on to the "inferior" partner

"The princess became controversial because of her **morganatic** marriage."

morkrumbo   the making up by bureaucrats of impressive-sounding job titles for mundane positions

> "I'm not impressed by **morkrumbo**, since what someone really *does* is to me much more important than what his job title *says* he does."

mot juste   (mō•ZYUST)   the perfect word or phrase; precisely apt expression; an expression or word that conveys precisely the right shade of meaning

> "The skillful writer had little difficulty finding the **mot juste**."

mungo   one who retrieves valuables from garbage

> "The skilled **mungo** is able to perceive what is useful in things that most others regard as useless."

muricide   (MYERicīd)   killing of mice

> "I got my cat partly for its ability to commit **muricide**."

musculade   to mutter under one's breath

> "Whenever he wanted to criticize his boss, he would **musculade** his words rather than address his boss directly."

mycterism   (MIKteriz'm)   derision or sarcasm that is somewhat veiled

"Whenever I am the object of **mycterism**, I ask the perpetrators to unveil their insults."

myrmidon (*MER*mudon), **pandour** (PANdur) a brutal, marauding soldier

"We must assume that, in war, every army has its share of **myrmidons**."

mythoclast (MITHuklast) destroyer of myths

"The nineteenth-century agnostic Robert Ingersoll held that **mythoclasts** were serving truth by clearing out weeds."

mythomania (mithuMĀnēu) an abnormal propensity for telling lies (and believing them)

"Politicians can tell so many lies that they may fall into **mythomania**, in which they cannot distinguish between truth and fiction."

mythopoeic (mithuPĒik) causing a myth to arise

"The story about Prometheus shows great **mythopoeic** imagination."

N

nephrolithotomy (NEFru • liTHOTumē) surgical removal of a stone from the kidney

"The severe pain you're experiencing is caused by a kidney stone, which we'll have to remove by performing an immediate **nephrolithotomy**."

nepimnemic (nepimNĒmik) a subconscious childhood memory

"His **nepimnemic** experience with his stepfather, which he had blocked completely from his consciousness, was the cause of most of his depression."

For information about the *mn* part of this word, see "ideomania."

nesiote (NĒsēōt) living on an island

"Many viewers were so tired of the **nesiote** people on 'Gilligan's Island' that they wanted them to be rescued—immediately."

The *nes* root meaning "island" also appears in the names of several island groupings, such as "Indonesia" and "Polynesia."

Newsthink exaggeration, misquotation, and other dubious techniques used by some members of the news media to create news

"The organization Accuracy in Media insists that the distorting power of **Newsthink** is greater than most people realize."

nidifugous (niDIFyugus) leaving the nest soon after birth

"People, unlike some birds, aren't **nidifugous**, but need much training before they can 'leave the nest.'"

nikhedonia (nikhēDŌNyu) pleasure derived from anticipating success

"I think that **nikhedonia** is often more enjoyable than success itself."

nit an insect with incomplete metamorphosis

"Like a **nit**, he had not achieved a complete metamorphosis."

niter (NĪter) gunpowder used for mining

"When using **niter**, people need to be extremely careful unless they want to be hit by falling or flying debris."

noa (NŌu) pertaining to a milder word or expression, such as "gosh," "darn," "shoot," or "phooey," used in place of one considered profane or vulgar

"He preferred **noa** expressions to their harsh counterparts."

nosology (nōSOLujē) classification of diseases

"Dr. Thomas Szasz has questioned much of the **nosology** of psychiatry, which, according to him, commonly identifies problems in living, such as poor self-management skills, as 'mental illnesses.'"

nosomania (nōzōMĀNyu) incorrect belief of a patient that he has a certain disease

"It can be extremely difficult to disabuse a patient of **nosomania**, especially when the patient has some interest served by having others believe he or she is ill."

nostomania (nostuMĀNyu) a compulsion to return home

"Her sojourn in Hollywood had been such a great disappointment and so highly disillusioning that her **nostomania** was now all-consuming."

nostrificate   (NOStrifukāt)   to accept as one's own

"People need to **nostrificate** all their possessions, even their faults."

noun-banging, nounspeak   the excessive clustering of nouns, especially to form abstract phrases, as in "missile guidance center personnel office equipment maintenance"

"Because his speech was densely packed with contiguous nouns, which had little or no adjectival support, Henry Kissinger was accused of **noun-banging**."

novation   substitution of a new legal obligation for an old one

"As a result of the **novation**, I had a different creditor."

nucleomitophobia   fear of nuclear weapons

"**Nucleomitophobia** is far less prevalent now that the Soviet Union has fallen."

nudiustertian   (n*u*dē • uST*ER*shē′n),   **pridian** (PRIDēun)   pertaining to the day before yesterday

"The **nudiustertian** incidents were now simply a bad memory."

O

obtected   enclosed in a shell

"She lived in her house as if she were **obtected**, rarely leaving that safe and familiar environment."

ocelli   (ōSELī)   insect eyes

"She told us that some insects have so many hundreds of **ocelli** that they'd go bankrupt if they ever had to buy glasses."

ochlocracy   (okLOKrusē)   government by a mob or by the lowest of the people

"Plato viewed democracy as **ochlocracy**, in which mobs—'the many'—showed little respect for reason."

For information about the *ochlo* root, see "viaticum."

oikonisus   (*oi*KONisus)   an urge to start a family

"**Oikonisus** was their reason for deciding not to use birth control."

The odd-looking *oik* part of this word is actually related to some not-so-odd English words, all of which have some connection with "settling," "neighborhood," or "inhabiting." We have, for example, "parish" (from *paroikia*, "beside house"; hence, "neighbor," or "stranger," ultimately "a community"), "parochial," "villa" (related to Latin *vicus*, meaning "hamlet"), "village," "vicinity," "villain" (originally a farmer, hence uncivil), and "bailiwick" (dwelling—hence, district—of the bailiff).

We also have words related to managing, in the sense that settling down usually involves managing one's home. Hence, "ecology" (one's environs; originally *oecology*), "ecumenical" (originally *oecumenical*), and "economics" (home economics, for example).

olid   (OLid)   having a strong scent

"Because the perfume was **olid**, everyone noticed it."

omnies   in broadcasting, background sound of crowd noises

"Judging by the **omnies**, we mistakenly thought that there were a number of people listening to the disc jockey right at the broadcast station."

onychophagy   (oniKOFujē)   the habit of biting one's fingernails

"Before he went to the manicurist, he trimmed his nails by the nervous habit of **onychophagy**."

For information about the *onycho* root, see "exungulate." For information about the *phagy* root, see "geophagia."

oofle the attempt to find out the name of a person whose name you should know but cannot remember

"The **oofle** didn't work, and she ended up getting not the man's name but the story of his life."

ophthalmospintherism (ofTHALmu • SPINtheriz'm) the sensation of seeing spots before one's eyes

"Were those sparks I believe I saw real or was I suffering from **ophthalmospintherism**?"

opposable capable of being placed opposite something else

"Without an **opposable** thumb, we wouldn't have been able to create most of our technology."

opsablepsia (opsuBLEPsēu) the tendency not to look into another's eyes

"If you want to make a good impression on people, you'll need to make eye contact, fighting against any tendency toward **opsablepsia**."

opsigamy (opSIGumē) marriage late in life

127

"Since she had heard that early marriages often don't last, she went to the opposite extreme with her **opsigamy** in her eightieth year."

The main roots of the word are *opsi*, meaning "late," and *gamy*, meaning "marriage." For information about the *gamy* root, see "digamy."

opsimath   (OPsumath)   one who has learned late in life

"Many authors are **opsimaths**, not blooming intellectually until they are well over fifty years old."

The *math* part of this word is precisely the same root as that of "mathematics." It comes from the Greek, *mathein*, meaning "to learn." Ultimately it is descended from the Indo-European root, *men*, which pertains to "the mind" and "processes of thinking." Note, "mathematics" is related to the Sanskrit *manas* ("mind") plus *dadhāti* ("he puts," or "he places"). For information about other derivatives of the *men* root, see "ideomania."

orthoepy   (*OR*thuwepē)   correct pronunciation

"**Orthoepy** repays study since it is embarrassing to mispronounce words."

osculant   (OSkyulunt)   having certain characteristics in common, especially as one intermediate thing relates to two otherwise unrelated things

"The husband and wife were as different as night and day, except for their **osculant** habit of wanting to have the last word, which made for seemingly never-ending arguments."

For information about the *os* root, see "aboral."

O.S.S. an *o*bligatory *s*ex *s*cene—the expected erotic passage in a conventional novel (sometimes called a "pornopatch")—a publishing term that can also apply to a movie

"Many readers, who are used to sexual openness, demand an **O.S.S.** in almost every novel."

ossa (OSu) movable mountain (mythological)

"This mountain is an **ossa**, quite movable if we all work together to resolve the problem."

ossify (OSufī) to become rigid or fixed in outlook or attitudes

"Sometimes personal preferences **ossify** into prejudices."

Literally this word means "to make or become bone." After all, bone is indeed rigid.

The major root is from the ancient Indo-European word for bone, *oss* or *ost*. This same root appears in "**ost**eopathy" and "**ost**eoporosis," both words relating to bone disease. Oysters, which have hard, bonelike shells, get their name from the Greek word for bone, osteon.

The island called Key West is not related to a door key or to the direction west. Rather "Key West" is the bastardized Anglicized version of the original Spanish word for the islands, Cayo **Hues**o, "island of bones."

oubliation   (*u*blēĀshun)   the act or process of disposing of unwanted persons in a castle's well (the oubliette)

"Opponents of the King would sometimes suffer **oubliation**, never to be heard from again."

outlier   (*out*līer)   one whose office is not at home; one who sleeps outdoors

"The **outlier** spent over one hour commuting to work each day."

P

palimpsest (PALim[p]sest) a parchment or tablet that has been written on or engraved more than once

"The professor maintained that, unlike a **palimpsest**, the mind's experiences are not erasable."

palinoia (paliNOIu) the compulsion to do something repeatedly until it is perfect

"The tennis trainer told his pupil to hit the ball against the wall so many times that the practice becomes virtually a **palinoia**."

panarchy (PANawrkē) rule over the entire universe

"According to many, God's rule is a **panarchy**."

panchreston (panKREStun) an oversimple thesis that is too broad to cover adequately its subject

"His theory was so broad that it was simply another untestable, unfalsifiable **panchreston**."

pancosmism (panKOZmiz′m)   belief that nothing exists beyond the material universe

"The theologian rejected Marx's **pancosmism**, which excludes supernatural events."

pandect   a book covering an entire subject, such as the laws of a country

"Although he knew enough to write a **pandect** on his subject, he chose instead to write relatively short articles."

pandemonium   the capital of hell

"The most lawless part of that rough neighborhood was the city's **pandemonium**, where vicious people assembled to plan their sins."

pandiculation (panDIKyu•LĀshun)   yawning and stretching at the same time

"Neither yawning nor stretching by itself is as pleasurable as **pandiculation**."

panoptic (puNOPtik)   allowing a view of all parts, as a panoptic aerial photograph of a city

"The warden held that we need prisons that afford wardens **panoptic** views."

paralogize (puRALugīz)   to draw illogical conclusions from a set of facts

"The philosopher Immanuel Kant argued that, if reason attempted to deal with theses beyond our possible experience, reason would **paralogize**, leading to self-contradictions."

paraph (PARuf)   flourish at the end of a signature

"Originally, people added **paraphs** to their signatures to prevent forgery."

paraphasia (peruFĀzyu)   habitual inclusion of extremely inappropriate words or phrases in one's speech

"Her **paraphasia** was so bad that she would rarely utter more than five words without using at least one nonsensical word."

parapherna (peruFERnu)   the part of a woman's property that remains legally hers after marriage

"Consider your dignity your **parapherna**; no matter how your marriage ends up, you can retain that throughout your life—your former husband will have no say in the matter."

parapraxis (peruPRAKSis)   a faulty action, memory block, or speech error, as a slip of the tongue

"The woman said that she didn't mean to step on my toe, but I sensed that this apparent **parapraxis** was intentional."

parenteral (parENTerul)   not entering the body by means of absorption from the intestine, as a drug by injection

"If he will not open his mouth to eat his food, we can find other, perhaps **parenteral**, means of nourishing him."

parhelion (pawrHĒLēun) a mock sun—specifically, a halolike light seen at a point opposite the sun

"The evangelist painted herself as a great savior, but most could see through her phony talk and gimmickry; the 'guiding light' that she claimed to be was, at best, a **parhelion**."

pathetic fallacy, anthropopathism (anthruPOputhiz´m) the attributing of human emotions or characteristics to inanimate objects or to nature, as in "the cruel sea," "brave snowdrops," "devouring flame."

"Our logician pointed out that attributing human emotions to inanimate objects, though it is called a **pathetic fallacy**, is not a fallacy but a poetic figure."

pathocryptia (pathōKRIPtēu) unwillingness to talk about one's illness

"Her **pathocryptia** made it difficult for the doctor to discover the exact nature of her illness; she seemed to be ashamed to reveal the details of her medical problems."

pathodyxia (pathōDIKsēu) excessive talkativeness about one's illness

"When we innocently asked the people how they

were, we were treated to an unending list of medical symptoms, eagerly trotted out by people who came to be known for their **pathodyxia**."

peccavi   (peKOvē)   a confession of wrongdoing

"No mere **peccavi** would ever be sufficient to ease the pain he had inflicted upon his family."

peculium   (piK[Y]*U*lēum)   a private or exclusive possession

"The salary of a Roman soldier was exclusive property and so constituted his **peculium**."

pedant   (PĒD′nt)   a narrow-minded person or teacher who overemphasizes rules or trivial details

"The **pedant** insisted that, to be a good writer, 'You've got to—in every instance—avoid splitting infinitives.' "

pedicab   a three-wheeled vehicle moved by pedaling

"The **pedicab** driver prefers his vehicle to taxicabs, since he gets plenty of exercise and doesn't have any gasoline bills."

pelagianism   (piLĀJuniz′m)   belief in the basic goodness of nature, including human nature

"Anyone who believes in original sin and the innate depravity of people will continue to regard **pelagianism** as heretical."

pelf   mere wealth

"J. Paul Getty was a billionaire with more than enough **pelf**, yet he said that he would have given everything away for one happy marriage."

peripeteia   (peru•puTĒu)   a dramatic turnaround in the action of a literary work

"In the novel, the **peripeteia** was ushered in by the death of the protagonist's father, on whom the protagonist was emotionally and financially dependent."

perissotomist   (periSOTumist)   a   knife-happy   surgeon

"Although much surgery is unnecessary, there are many **perissotomists** who think, and want others to think, otherwise."

peristalsis   (peruSTOLsis)   rhythmic   contractions progressing in one direction along a muscular tube, as the intestines, and propelling the contents along it and toward the point of expulsion

"Her friend claimed that drinking coffee often promotes **peristalsis**, which in turn promotes defecation."

For information about the *sta* part of this word, see "instauration."

pernoctation (pernokTĀshun)   a night-long vigil

"The night before the sentence was carried out, activists opposed to the death penalty held a **pernoctation**."

petard (piTAWRD)   an explosive device formerly used for making breaches in walls and gates

"His inflammatory comment, like a **petard**, was responsible for the ensuing explosion."

petracide   the destruction of ancient stone buildings or monuments

"The historical presevationist held that **petracide** should be punished almost as severely as homicide."

pettifogger (PETē•fogu[r])   an incompetent lawyer who handles minor cases

"She needs a competent lawyer with extensive experience in important cases, not some **pettifogger**."

philippize   to speak or write under bribery or corrupt influence

"He wasn't speaking from his heart but was **philippizing**."

philogyny (fiLOJunē)   love of women

"Always near a beautiful woman, James Bond was known for his **philogyny**."

philophronesis (FILō·frōNĒsis)   the use of gentle speech or humble submission to calm someone who is angry

"When the Bible recommends offering a kind word to turn away wrath, it is recommending **philophronesis**."

philopolemical (FILō·puLEMik'l)   loving to fight; loving war

"The politician held that while Americans aren't a **philopolemical** people, they will fight for what they deeply believe in."

philoprogenitive (FILō·prōJENutiv), **polyphiloprogenitive**, **proletaneous** (prōluTANēus)   being fond of one's children or of children in general; having many children

"She was so **philoprogenitive** that she had seven children and wanted more."

"The senator held that in this country, where birth control is widely available, there is no excuse for poor people to be **proletaneous**."

For information about the *gen* part of this word, see "gnomon."

philotheoparoptesism   (filuTHĒu •puROPtusiz′m)
the offering of human sacrifice for religious reasons

> "**Philotheoparoptesism** used to be a common fea-
> ture of many religions, but today most religious
> people argue that the practice is nothing more than
> murder in a religious context."

philoxenist   (fiLOKsunist)   a lover of hospitality to
strangers

> "Every person at our soup kitchen is a **philoxenist**
> who enjoys helping strangers even more than help-
> ing friends."

photophobe   an organ or organism that thrives in the
dark or turns away from the light

> "Since vampires are **photophobes**, they sleep dur-
> ing the day."

phrasemonger   (frāzmong*er*)   one prone to quoting
the words of others, replete with clichés, platitudes, and
secondhand expressions

> "Excellent writers aren't **phrasemongers** but pride
> themselves instead on their ability to create original
> colorful expressions."

phronesis (frōNĒsis)   wisdom in choosing aims and in the ways of achieving these aims

"The philosopher urged his followers to pursue not only theoretical knowledge but also **phronesis**, which is necessary for wise living."

phthisozoics (thisōZŌiks)   destroying harmful animals

"The practice of **phthisozoics** is necessary to prevent our being overrun by rabid and other diseased animals."

physiognomy (fizēOGnumē)   facial   features   regarded as clues to character

"His **physiognomy** had the contours of a person who suffered many misfortunes with admirable patience."

For information about the *gn* part of this word, see "gnomon."

pianteric (pēunTERik)   fattening food

"Their taste in food ran in the direction of such **pianteric** as baklava dipped in hot fudge."

piebald (PĪb*aw*ld)   having black and white spots

"They prefer **piebald** horses to monochromatic ones."

piloerection   (PĪlō·iREKshun)   hair standing on end, often a sign of fear

> "His fright was so intense that the resulting **pilo-erection** actually knocked off his cap."

polygraphy   (puLIGrufē)   notable literary productivity and variety, applying particularly to the body of work of prolific and versatile writers

> "Isaac Asimov, who wrote over four hundred books on several subjects, was widely praised for his almost unmatched **polygraphy**."

The main roots of the word are *poly*, meaning "many," and *graph*, meaning "writing."

Interestingly, abbreviated forms of the *poly* root are found in several words containing "pl," such as "**pl**enty," "re**pl**enish," "**pl**ural," "**pl**us," "sur**pl**us," "**pl**ethora," "re**pl**ete," "sup**pl**y," "de**pl**ete," and "com**pl**ete." The *poly* root has also given rise to linguistically related "f-l" words, such as "full," "fill," and "folks" ("many persons").

By the way, now that you know what polygraphy is, what do you suppose a polygraph is—a lie detector? Well, yes, but it's also a prolific or versatile writer!

polyhistorian, polymath   (POLēmath)   one who has mastered many fields of knowledge

> "Since we deeply admired the **polyhistorian** Isaac Asimov, who wrote over four hundred books on such diverse subjects as chemistry, Shakespeare, the

Bible, and science fiction, we were elated when he
consented to write the introduction to our book on
fundamentalism."

See also "flitwite."

polylemma   (POLē • lemu)   a situation in which there
are three or more unpleasant alternatives

"Whether you are in a dilemma or a **polylemma**,
you are faced with unpleasant options."

polysemant   (polēSĒmunt)   a single word having a
variety of meanings

"We are told that 'set' is the **polysemant** with a
greater variety of meanings than any other word in
the English language."

polysemy   (POLē • sēmē)   a variety of meanings or
senses

"Because the language in the Bible is marked by
polysemy, different interpretations are not only
possible but expected."

preterist   (PREDurist)   one who is fond of reliving
the past

"I have no time for the nostalgic stories of some
preterist."

primipara (priMIPuru)   a woman who has borne only one child

"She has had so many problems with her one child that she is likely to remain a **primipara**."

probang (PRŌbang)   a rod inserted into the esophagus to remove obstructions

"You'll need a **probang** to dislodge all those words you're going to be eating when I prove you wrong."

prodromal (PRODrum'l)   related to the first signs of a disease

"The learned sociologist said that the breakdown of the American family is **prodromal**, foreshadowing ever-increasing crime, drug abuse, violence, and other ills of society."

prodrome (PRŌdrōm)   a warning symptom

"His persistent cough and shortness of breath are **prodromes** of more serious respiratory problems."

pro forma   done according to or for the sake of form

"Although you'll need your teacher's signature for this project, I assure you that the signature is simply **pro forma**."

progeria (prōJIRēu)   premature aging (also called Hutchinson-Gilford syndrome)—a rare congenital disorder of childhood in which the rapid onset of physical changes typical of old age usually produces death before the age of twenty

> "Old as it is, the earth is nonetheless suffering **progeria** at the hands of an environmentally careless humanity."

> "A postmortem examination will be carried out on . . . a nine-year old girl who died of a disease that gave her the physical characteristics of a ninety-year-old woman. Norma . . . was the second member of her family to suffer from **progeria**" (*The Guardian*, January 13, 1969).

The main roots of this word are *pro*, meaning "early" or "before," and *ger*, meaning "old age."

pseudologue (S*U*Dul*awg*)   a pathological liar

> "When it was discovered that the prosecution's star witness was a **pseudologue**, everyone knew that the state had lost the case."

pseudomnesia (s*u*domNĒZyu)   "memory" for things that never happened

> "His **pseudomnesia** allowed him to believe that his wife had told him to go to the store for groceries, for, he reasoned, had it not been for her persistent demands to do so, he would never have gotten into an accident on his way to the store."

For information about the *mn* part of this word, see "ideomania".

pseudothyrum (sudōTHĪrum) a secret or private entrance

"This is our **pseudothyrum**, through which you can always get inside without anyone else seeing you."

psilanthropism (sĭLANthrupiz′m) the belief that Christ was an ordinary human being

"Although Thomas Jefferson regarded Jesus as a great moral teacher, he didn't regard Jesus as divine but subscribed instead to **psilanthropism**."

The term comes from the Greek combining form *psil-* or *psilo-*, which literally means "to rub" or "to wipe," and from the Greek *anthropos* (human being), the idea being that rubbing off some divine disguise or claim reveals a mere human being. The term refers to a heretical doctrine within Christianity, namely, that Jesus was a fully human being and not at all divine. Unitarianism, for example, is technically based on psilanthropism because its adherents deny the existence of the Trinity and regard Jesus as fully human.

psilosopher (sĭLOSufer) a superficial philosopher

"The professor held that there are only a few great philosophers within the Western tradition and that the rest are only nominal philosophers or **psilosophers**."

psittacism (SITusiz′m) mindless, repetitive, parrotlike speech

"To the unreligious woman, reciting prayers in church was simply **psittacism**."

pygalgia (pīGALgēu) soreness in the buttocks

"I'd say he's a pain in the neck, but he's a **pygalgia**, which means he is painful farther down."

pygmalionism (pigMĀLyuniz'm) condition of falling in love with one's own creation

"There is no place for **pygmalionism** now that conditions have changed and the institutions that were once useful and effective must be completely redesigned or even discarded."

The term is from Pygmalion, the legendary king and sculptor of Cyprus who fell in love with the statue that he made of a woman, and in honor of whose request Aphrodite gave the statue life.

"Pygmalionism" can also refer to sexual response to a statue or other representation.

Pyrrhic (PĪRik) **victory** a victory that costs more than it gains

"The Democrat held that we won a **Pyrrhic victory** over the former Soviet Union, since we ignored our worsening roads, education, and crime in order to bankrupt them in the arms race."

pysma the use of a series of short questions that require different answers for dramatic effect

"Skilled in interrogation, the lawyer effectively used **pysma** in the cross-examination."

Q

Q.E.D. (*q*uod *e*rat *d*emonstrandum)   as has just been shown or proved

"You'll need to prove your thesis before you're entitled to write **Q.E.D.**"

quadragenarian (kwodru-juNĀRēun)   a person who is more than forty but less than fifty years old

"Close to fifty years old, many rock stars of the 1960s are **quadragenarians**."

"Quadragenarian" comes from the Latin *quadraginta*, literally meaning "four (*quadra*), ten times (*ginta*)." Note that a period of forty days, such as Lent, is called the "quadragesima." And "quarantine" also literally refers to a period of forty days, the time originally designated for the quarantine of ships.

quadraliteralism (kwodruLITeruliz′m)   use of taboo (four-letter) words

"Mr. Wright is one of the few eminently successful comedians who needn't resort to **quadraliteralism** or any other shock tactics."

R

recension scholarly editorial revision

"The journal will accept your article but only after **recension**, since some of the language must be refined."

receptary (RESup•terē) a recipe collection; accepted as fact but unproved

"The philosopher admitted that God's existence is **receptary** but held that popular beliefs have often been erroneous beliefs."

recrudescence (rēkr*u*DES′nts) a reopening of an old wound; reappearance of a previous disease

"When the economy worsened, there was a **recrudescence** of lynchings."

rectigrade moving in a straight line

"We must not be sidetracked; we must take **rectigrade** steps toward our goals."

recumbentibus (rekumBENTibus) a knockdown blow

"When Senator Joseph McCarthy was sharply asked whether he still had any sense of decency, he received a **recumbentibus** from which he never recovered."

For information about the *cumb* part of this word, see "couvade."

redhibition (red[h]uBISHun) the return of defective merchandise

"Since it seems as though everything I buy is defective, I think I go to stores more often for **redhibition** than for making purchases."

reductive fallacy the fallacy of reducing a complex issue or problem to one oversimple thing or aspect

"When the psychoanalyst argued that all action is motivated by a desire for sex or death, he was accused of committing the **reductive fallacy**."

reefer a front-page notice in a newspaper that refers the reader to a story on an inside page

"Newspaper people like using **reefers** because they encourage people to read beyond the front page."

rhinestone vocabulary words and phrases chosen by a speechwriter to appeal to a particular group, as funeral metaphors for a speech at a funeral directors' meeting.

"When speaking to libertarians, the politician's **rhinestone vocabulary** included 'individualism'; but when she spoke to evangelical Christians, her vocabulary contained instead 'family values.'"

rhinophonia (rīnuFŌNēu) strong nasality in one's voice

"The linguist maintained that many blacks perceive white people as having nasalized voices and that they coined the word 'honky' to refer to that **rhinophonia**."

rhinorrhea (rīnuRĒu) runny nose

"His **rhinorrhea** prompted him constantly to take out his handkerchief and wipe his nose."

rhyparography (rīpuROGrufē) painting of or writings on depressing or sordid subjects; the act of painting or writing about depressing or sordid subjects.

"Some painters love depicting hangings, murders, and other morbid subjects fit principally for **rhyparography**."

rhytiphobia (ritiFŌbēu) fear of getting wrinkles

"That face cream is advertised especially to older women whose **rhytiphobia** might drive them to pay high prices to try to remove wrinkles."

rhytiscopia (ritiSCOPēu) an abnormal preoccupation with facial wrinkles

"His concern over the wrinkles on his face borders on **rhytiscopia**."

The *scop* in "rhytiscopia" comes from the ancient root *spek* ("see," "regard"), which has also given rise to such words as "**spec**tator," "su**spect**," "ex**pect**," "frontis**piece**," "**spec**ial," and "**spy**." By the linguistic process known as metathesis, *spek* also came to be pronounced-"skep," from which came most of our *-scope* words, such as "micro**scope**" and "horo**scope**." It is also related to "**bi**shop" and "epi**scop**al" (literally, "watching over"). "Bishop" is, in fact, a shortening of "epi**scop**al" (*piscop* = bishop).

risibility (rizuBILutē) the inclination to laugh

"Her **risibility** is sometimes hazardous to her career, as when she laughed at her boss after he tripped over the wastebasket."

S

savate (saVAT)   fighting with feet and hands

"He preferred **savate** to pure boxing because he had developed a very powerful kick."

Schadenfreude (SHOd′n • fro*i*du)   enjoyment of another's misfortune

"If you see someone slip on a banana peel, you might well experience **Schadenfreude**."

schatchen (SHOT*ch*en)   a Jewish marriage broker

"The Jewish man insisted that he didn't need some **schatchen** picking out a bride for him."

schesis (SKĒsis)   mocking another's accent or manner

"The radio talk show host's **schesis** annoyed many of the liberals of whom he often made fun."

schizothemia (skizōTHĒmēu) digression of a long reminiscence

sciamachy (sīOMukē) the act of fighting with an imaginary enemy or a shadow

"I tried to convince him that he was engaged not in a real battle but in a **sciamachy** prompted by unrealistic fears."

The -*machy* part of this word is probably a descendant of *magh*, the same ancient root that has given us "may," "might," "mighty," "machine," "Amazon," and "magic." All are related to power: the **migh**ty and those with **might** have power; one who **may** is able and has been given the power, or the permission, to do something; **mach**ines give us the power to do more things more quickly; "-machy" words pertain to battles, or power struggles (see also "logomachy"); the **Amazons** were female warriors; and **magic** is a mysterious power.

sciolism (SĪuliz′m) superficial show of knowledge

"Some people who know very little resort to **sciolism** to display the little they do know."

scut a very short tail such as that of a hare or a deer

"A Doberman pinscher doesn't have a natural **scut**, but its tail is often surgically shortened."

Second Coming type extraordinarily large newspaper type

"Although the breakout of the war produced numerous front-page articles with headlines in **Second Coming type**, the subsequent opposition to the war seldom garnered more than a few third- or fourth-page stories with nearly microscopic headlines."

secundipara (sekunDIPuru) a woman who has borne two children

"She told us that she had one boy and one girl and was happy to remain a **secundipara**."

sedentarize (seDENturiz) to take up, or cause to take up, a permanent residence after a life of nomadic wandering

"A roaming biker, he wasn't the sort of person who could easily be **sedentarized** and domesticated."

sematic (siMATik) serving as a warning to enemies, as the conspicuous colors of some poisonous animals

"His **sematic** scowl and shout were enough to scare away the timid racoon."

serein (suRAWN) rain at sunset

"Because of the clear sky, we didn't anticipate the **serein** last evening."

serendipitous (serunDIPudus) pertaining to the accidental discovery of pleasant things not sought

"Many scientific discoveries are **serendipitous**."

"The English teacher suggested that, since 'fortuitous' properly refers only to chance, not to good fortune, and since 'fortunate' refers only to good fortune, not to chance, one should simply use the word **'serendipitous'** to describe that which is both fortunate and fortuitous."

shlep   to carry with difficulty

"The old woman had some close calls as she **shlepped** her six-month-old granddaughter near the edge of the Grand Canyon."

sigogglin   (siGOGlin)   tilted to the right, as, for example, a leaning barn

"Politically, she's a centrist who is occasionally **sigogglin**."

sinistrodextral   (SINistru • DEKstr'l)   moving   from left to right

"From the 1960s to the 1990s the U.S. moved in a **sinostrodextral** political path."

sisyphean   (sisuFĒun)   endless, unavailing, and fruitless labor

"Eliminating all bigotry would be a **sisyphean** task."

sitomania   (sītōMĀnēu)   obsession with food or with eating

"They need to force themselves to be interested in many things other than food if they are ever to overcome their **sitomania**."

For information about the *sito* root, see "aristology."

situs (SĪtus) the original or proper position

"Palestine is the **situs** of their Semitic ancestry."

sizzle seller a product that sells because of slick marketing rather than content or quality

"That novel, a **sizzle seller**, won't be remembered even two years from now."

skein (skān) circumstances or undertakings easily twisted or mixed up

"Through her own poor choices, she has gotten herself into a **skein** of difficulties that will not easily be unraveled."

slops distillery mash after the alcohol has been removed; liquid waste; waste food used to feed pigs or other animals

"They want jobs so that they can eat decent food instead of the **slops** others leave."

The word "slops" comes from "cowslip," the slippery, sloppy stuff more familiarly known as "cow dung."

slurvian American language marked by carelessly slurred pronunciations such as "gimme," "c'mon," and "d'ju"

"Many people in the United States speak **slurvian**, taking neither the time nor the effort to enunciate their words."

somniloquism (somNILukwiz′m) talking in one's sleep

"His **somniloquism** revealed to his wife some of his infidelities."

sophistry (SOFistrē) fallacious reasoning

"When people try to rationalize an indefensible view, they often resort to **sophistry**."

sophophobia (sofōFŌbēu) fear or dislike of learning

"The professor accused the habitually absent student of **sophophobia**."

sortie (SAWRtē) aircraft on a single military mission

"The battle-weary pilot had flown so many **sorties** that he had long since lost count."

soteria (sōTIRēu) possessions that give a sense of peace and security

"Her **soteria** included a book of inspirational poems and pictures of her family."

sound   to test the depth of water

"Our crew must **sound** the bottom to ensure that there is enough water for our vessel."

spanogyny   (spaNOJunē)   scarcity of women

"When he moved to a remote part of Alaska, he soon noticed its **spanogyny** as he looked for female companionship."

spansule   a timed-release capsule

"She took a **spansule** for her cold, hoping that it would give her several hours of relief."

sphygmomanometer   (SFIGmō • muNOMut*er*)   an instrument used to measure blood pressure

"The bodybuilder's left arm was too large for the **sphygmomanometer**."

In "sphygmomanometer," the meaning of *meter* is obvious: it pertains to measuring.

The *sphygmo* part is far less obvious. The only common word it's related to is "asphyxiate," literally "not (*a-*) beating": when your heart's not beating, you're not breathing.

The middle of this word, *mano*, comes from the Greek *manos*, meaning "loose," "sparse," "infrequent." The blood pressure-measuring instrument operates on a principle similar to that of a manometer, which measures the pressure of gases and vapors. So what's the connection? Well, gases and vapors are, in a sense, loose and sparse (*manos*).

stereognosis (sterēogNŌsis) the ability to perceive similarities and differences in the material qualities (such as size, weight, and shape) of objects by touching or lifting them

"His powers of **stereognosis** were so impressive that he could tell us the weight of a box simply by touching it."

For information about the *gn* part of this word, see "gnomon."

sternutation (st*erny*uTĀshun) noise produced by sneezing

"The teacher's loud **sternutation** prompted the students to blurt out 'Bless you!'"

stillatitious (stiluTIshus) falling in drops

"Rain is **stillatitious** water from clouds."

stipple to paint, engrave, or draw with dots instead of lines

"He **stippled** part of the painting to produce a softly graded shadow."

stomatic (stuMATik)   pertaining to the mouth

"The native's **stomatic** ornamentation included a painful-looking assortment of beads and rings."

strabismus (struBIZmus)   the condition of being cross-eyed

"The interviewer tried to look the interviewee straight in the eye but had difficulty because of her **strabismus**."

The *strab* part of this word comes from the original Indo-European root, *stebh*, meaning "turn," or "twist." This root has given us such words as "apostrophe" (a turning away: both a turned-away punctuation mark and an addressing of a person not present, or turned away), "catastrophe" (literally, an overturning), "boustrophedon" (writing in which the lines run alternately from left to right, then right to left, and so on; originally, the turning of an ox [*bous*; hence, bovine] pulling a plow), "streptococcus" (bacterium shaped like a twisted chain), "strobe," and "stroboscope."

stratocracy (struTOKrusē)   government by the military

"We have a civilian commander-in-chief as a check against a tyrannical **stratocracy**."

suborn (suBORN)   to hire or otherwise encourage someone to commit a crime; to bribe an official

"The restaurant owner tried to **suborn** the city food inspector to overlook the rats and roaches."

succubus (SUKyubus) a female demon supposed to have sex with men while they are asleep

"Although men of the medieval period claimed that they were attacked in their sleep by a **succubus**, many people nowadays dismiss that claim as a product of dreams and overactive imaginations."

For information about the *cub* part of this word, see "couvade."

sudd a temporary dam

"The drug war is but a **sudd**, and a partial one at that; the effort to stop the flow of drugs is sisyphean."

suggestio falsi (sugJESchēō FAWLsē) an intentionally misleading comment; a statement that easily leads the reader or listener to a false inference

"When the oil company advertised that its gasoline contained 'platformate,' it was guilty of a **suggestio falsi**, since it implied that this ingredient was unusual rather than standard in gasoline."

suitorcide that which destroys the chance of a suitor

"His arriving late and then calling her dress ugly was **suitorcide**."

Suitors pur**sue**, or follow, their hoped-for mate. Things that follow one another are said to be in **se-que**nce. Whatever follows "the first" is said to be the **sec**ond." A **sect** is composed of persons who follow a particular **set** of beliefs. Ob**sequ**ies are the rites that follow death. An ob**sequ**ious person dutifully bends to—follows—the will of another. A **suit**e of rooms, a **suit** of cards, and wardrobe of **suit**s are all sets, systematically arranged, one following the other.

So all of the boldfaced parts of words in the preceding paragraph are related to a root that means "follow"— namely the Indo-European root, *seku*.

sypher   to join edge to edge to form an even surface, as of slant-edged boards

> "The carpenter's **syphering** was so precise that no one knew the floor had been damaged and then repaired."

163

T

tacenda   things better left unsaid

"We can't understand why people like to listen to
Howard Stern, since most of his distasteful attempts
at humor involve **tacenda**."

tachyauxesis   (TAKē • awgZĒsis)   in an organism, the
growth of a part at a faster rate than the whole

"We expect a baby's head to develop faster than,
say, its hands, since that form of **tachyauxesis** is
part of normal human development."

tachycardia   (takiKAWRDēu)   rapid heart rate

"He was so sensitive to caffeine that even one cup
of coffee would immediately induce a severe bout
of **tachycardia**."

The *card* part of this word comes from the Indo-
European root, *kerb*, meaning "heart." "Heart" itself is
the Germanic form of this root (remember, "k," "ch," and
"h" are related). From it we also have "cordial," "ac-

cord," "accordion," "concord," "discord," "courage," "record" (to call to mind; in a sense, written on or in the heart), and "cardinal." Cardinal was originally a door hinge, the heart or center of the door, and then, figuratively, the central point on which something hinges. (For example, the cardinal virtues, on which access to paradise hinges; the College of Cardinals, on whom the succession of the popes hinges.) From the cardinal's cap came the color cardinal; then from the color came the bird's name. See also "cardiomegaly."

tachydidaxy   (taki·dīDAKsē)   fast teaching

"They wanted the teacher to proceed at a slower, more leisurely pace but soon realized that **tachydidaxy** was her natural style."

tachyphagia   (takiFĀjēu)   extremely fast eating

"His **tachyphagia** was so severe that he almost inhaled his food."

For information about the *phag* part of this word, see "geophagia."

tare   the weight of the truck, box, wrapping paper, or other receptacle or material in which goods are packed or carried

"We can determine the **tare** of the truck by subtracting the weight of its goods from the gross weight of the loaded truck."

tatterdemalion (tat*er* • diMĀLyun)   a person dressed in ragged clothing

"The **tatterdemalion** asked for money to buy a sandwich."

tectonics   the art or science of building construction

"Since he was skilled in **tectonics**, he was concerned not only with the usefulness of the building but also with its artistry."

ted   to spread out for drying

"The gardener maintained that there is an art to **tedding** manure."

teleology (telēOLujē)   the doctrine that all things in nature are designed to serve a purpose

"Although the ancient philospher Aristotle and most medieval philosophers took **teleology** for granted, many modern thinkers reject the idea of cosmic purpose."

telephanous (telEFunus)   visible from a great distance

"The **telephanous** moon, though hundreds of thousands of miles away, sometimes appears to be just up the street."

telepheme   (TELufēm)   a telephone message

"Her message on the telephone, though not the least bit helpful, was certainly short and accurate: '**Telepheme**.'"

thestreen   last night

"She has a hangover today because she drank too much **thestreen**."

thimblerig   (THIMb'l • rig)   to cheat with simple sleight of hand, especially by using three shells or thimbles and a pea or other small object that is placed under one of the shells and moved around

"Those men are like dupes at a fair, **thimblerigged** into believing that they know where the pea is."

timocracy   (tĭMOKrusē)   government by the most honored people

"Most Americans don't expect a **timocracy** but expect instead rule by dishonorable people."

tinnitus   (tĭNĪtus)   ringing in the ear

"People can usually tell the difference between **tinnitus** and external ringing, as from a phone."

tintiddle   (TINtid'l)   a witty retort you wish you had made but thought of too late

"I hope that the **tintiddle** that occurred to me two hours after the debate will serve me in future debates."

tirocinium (tirōSINēm) a soldier's first battle

"For many American soldiers in Iraq, the fighting was their **tirocinium**."

topophobia (topōFŌbēu) stage fright

"The weather forecaster Willard Scott has said that his **topophobia** was so severe that he would vomit right before appearing on camera."

topopolitan (topōPOlitun) pertaining to a particular area; the opposite of cosmopolitan

"If our town is ever going to attract more business, we need to have a cosmopolitan rather than **topo-politan** imagination."

tranont to shift one's position, especially rapidly and stealthily

"Like a Special Forces soldier, the politician is skilled at **tranonting**, shifting his position with great subtlety."

trim to maintain neutrality between opposing parties

"Neither side wants us to **trim**; each wants us to favor it."

triphibious (trīFIBēus) able to operate on land, at sea, and in the air

"Schwarzkopf praised the army, navy, and air force, since he believed in each element of the triphibious military."

The *phi* part of "triphibious" really makes no sense. The *bio* part of the word relates to "living," as in "**bio**logy," or, in this case, "operating." And the *tri* part obviously means "three" (land, sea, and air). The *phi* part is there only to make the word resemble "amphibious," "able to live both on land and in water." The *phi* in *amphi-* is related to *bi*, a root for "two," or "both." So, in reality, "triphibious" should mean something like, "living both on land, in water, and in the air." As we said, the *phi* doesn't make sense!

trochal   (TRŌkʹl)   pertaining to wheels

"The tire merchant joked that he liked doughnuts because of their **trochal** shape."

troika   three in a governing group

"The minister submitted that the most famous **troika** in the world is composed of the Father, the Son, and the Holy Ghost."

tropophobia   (tropōFŌbēu)   fear of making changes

"Although few people are happy with the consequences of the drug war, policy analysts who suggest changes soon discover that they have excited many bureaucrats' **tropophobia**."

tu quoque (*TU* · KWŌkwē), **you-too-ism** a retort claiming that one's opponent is doing the very thing he or she criticizes in others (often introduced by the question, "Who are you to talk?")

"When I accused her of driving twenty miles over the speed limit, she responded with a **tu quoque**, and that was the end of that discussion."

U

unasinous (y*u*NAsinus) equally stupid

"Our representatives in Washington, D.C., are no more stupid than we are; we and they are **unasinous**."

unigeniture (y*u*niJENich*er*) being the only child

"Her **unigeniture** often made her feel lonely."

For information about the *gen* part of this word, see "gnomon."

uranography (y*er*uNOGruf*ē*) star mapping

"Although the astronomer and the astrologer were both interested in **uranography**, they made their star maps for sharply different reasons."

urbacity (*er*BAsit*ē*) excessive or foolish pride in one's city

"When Samuel Johnson said that people who are tired of London are tired of life, some people believed that he was guilty of geographical chauvinism, or **urbacity**."

usance (YUZ'nts) benefits from interest

"We were constantly exhorted to save money and to invest it so that we could enjoy the **usance**."

usufruct (YUzufrukt) the right to use or benefit from another's property short of harming or otherwise altering it

"My sister regards her use of my hair dryer as a **usufruct**."

This word comes from the Latin phrase *usus et fructus*—literally, "use and enjoy." *Fructus* is related to "fruit" (which is enjoyed) and "frugal" (related to the idea of a fruitful harvest, hence good value).

uxorilocal (ukSŌruLŌk'l) living with your wife's family

"In the TV series 'All in the Family,' Gloria's husband, Mike, often disliked his **uxorilocal** home, though he and Gloria couldn't afford to live away from her parents."

uxorovalence (ukSŌruVĀlints) state of being sexually potent with one's wife but not with other women

"Having moved to another city, I feel as if I'm the victim of a kind of **uxorovalence**, in which I now realize that I can't feel happy, fulfilled, and alive anywhere but in my own hometown."

V

vade mecum (vādē·MĒkum)   a favorite book one carries everywhere

"Our editor's **vade mecum** is Fowler's *Modern English Usage*."

venditation   displaying as if for sale

"We were shocked by the prostitute's brazen **venditation** of her body."

verbigeration (verbijuRĀshun)   the habit of frequently repeating favorite words or expressions

"Never varying his phrases, he would subject his listeners to his boring **verbigeration**."

viaticum (vīADikum)   an allowance for traveling expenses, or the money and provisions necessary for a journey

"We have a **viaticum** of seven hundred dollars for our trip to New York."

The *via* part of this word comes from the Indo-European root, *uegh*, meaning "to go," or "transport." It has given us "**och**locracy" (noisy crowds *moving* as a group; hence, mob rule), "**veh**icle" (from Latin *vehere*; remember, "v" and "u" are related), "in**veigh**" (to move against; hence, to protest vehemently), "in**vec**tive," "**vec**tor," "**way**" (manner, or direction, of movement; "u," "v," and "w" are related), "away," "always," "Norway" (the north way), "**wag**on," "**weigh**" (movement on the balance scale), "**vog**ue," (flow of fashion, trend), "voyage," "convoy," "convey," and "via."

vibrissae (vīBRISē)   the hair in the nostrils

"If you think he has hairy nostrils now, you should have seen him a year ago, before he started trimming his **vibrissae**."

virga (V*ER*gu)   rain that evaporates before it hits the ground

"The weather forecaster told us that we needn't carry umbrellas because the rain we'll get will be **virga**."

Virga is rain on the *verge* of hitting the ground. Indeed, "virga" and "verge" have a common origin in Latin *virga*, an obscure word meaning "rod" or "strip," the idea being that a strip is on the margin of something, a thin boundary line.

void in jigsaw puzzles, the space into which the rounded projection ("nub") is placed to form a "lock"

"When he told the group that a **'void'** is a 'female' jigsaw-puzzle piece, many people regarded his remark as sexist, though he didn't intend it to be."

W

winze   (winz)   a passage to various levels in a mine

   "The miner needed plenty of artificial light to move
   inside the **winze**."

withernam   (WI*the*rnom)   the action of taking something in reprisal for something else previously taken by
another

   "When the coach learned that we had taken their
   team's mascot in retaliation for their taking ours, he
   condemned our **withernam** by saying that two
   wrongs don't make a right."

It may seem strange, but the *with* part of this word
most nearly relates to the idea of being *against*, as it is,
after all, a reprisal. In fact, our word "with" originally
meant "against," which helps to explain such English
words and phrases as "**with**draw," "**with**stand," "contend
with," and "deal **with**."
   The *nam* part of this word means "take" and is related,
for example, to "**nim**ble" (nimble fingers are adept at

taking, or handling). For more information about the *nam/nim/nom* root, see "eunomy."

wog (wog)   food on the face

"The **wog** was so large that he had almost as much food on his face as he did in his stomach."

woodpusher   in chess, player of moderate or less than moderate ability

"The former world chess champion regarded most of his opponents not as worthy challengers but as **woodpushers**."

wordfact   the use of a highly specific and potentially damning label that results ultimately in acceptance of the label as factual: for example, the constant references to a particular group of people as "outcasts," "retarded," or "slow learners"

"We need always to examine our labels so that we do not stigmatize whole groups of people because of **wordfact**."

Y

yepsen cupping the hands so as to form a dish; the amount cupped hands can hold

"Each person went to the river to get a **yepsen** of water."

yestreen yesterday evening

"That was **yestreen**; this is tonight."

ylem (īlum) in philosophy, the primordial substance from which all things in the universe, including the elements, are derived

"She found it hard to believe that potato chips, hot dogs, and daytime television have all evolved from the **ylem**, the one ultimate principle."

This word is derived from the Greek *hylē*, which originally meant "wood," especially the wooden structures holding a ship together or holding up a building. *Hylē*, though, could also mean any material from which something could be made. Later, in philosophical circles, it came to mean the "substance" underlying reality, or the "matter" of which something is composed. "Hylism," for example, means "materialism."

Thesauro-Index

dysonogamia, horaphthia, opsigamy, opsimath, petracide, progeria, quadragenarian, rhytiphobia, rhytiscopia

AGGRESSION   see FIGHTING

AIR   (see also AIRPLANE, BREATHING, COVERING
[AS IN CLOUD], SMELL, SMOKING, STAR,
SUN)

aerobic, leeward, sortie, triphibious

AIRPLANE   (see also AIR, SPEED, TRAVEL, VE-
HICLE, WAR [AS IN AIR FORCE])

cocarde, dysrhythmia

ALCOHOL (see also DROP/DROPPING/DRIPPING,
LIQUID, MEDICINE, WATER, WILLPOWER
[AS IN ALCOHOLISM AND LACK OF
WILLPOWER/CONTROL])

slops

ALONE   see CROWD

ANGER   see LOVE

ANIMAL (see also CHILDREN, FOOD, GROWTH,
HOME, HUNTING, INSECTS, MAN/WOMAN,
NATURE, WASTE)

armentose, coffle, cynophilist, cynophobia, ephemeromorph, grike, guddle, hamble, holotype, laaba, muricide, phthisozoics

ANSWER   see QUESTION

ANT   see INSECT

ANXIETY   see FEAR

APOLOGY   see CONFESSION

APPRECIATION   see PRAISE

APPROPRIATE   see GOOD

APPROVAL   see PRAISE

ARGUMENT   (see also BELIEF, DECEPTION, FIGHT-
ING,   FRIEND/STRANGER,   KNOWLEDGE,

LOVE/HATE, OPPOSITENESS, PUNISHMENT,
QUESTION, REASON, SPEAKING, WARNING,
WORD)
ad ignorantiam, antistasis, apophasis, eristic, genetic
fallacy, hypocrisis, interpellation, maieutic, panchre-
ston, Q.E.D., reductive fallacy, sophistry, trim, tu
quoque/you-too-ism
ARITHMETIC   see MATH
ARM   see BODY
ART   (see also CULTURE, PAINTING, STATUE)
  Boeotian
ASS   see TAIL
ASTROLOGY   see STAR
ATMOSPHERE   see AIR
ATTACK   see FIGHTING
ATTENTION   see VISION or INDIFFERENCE
AUTOMOBILE   see VEHICLE

BABIES   see CREATIVITY or CHILD
BAD   see GOOD
BARKING   see ANIMAL
BASIC   see KNOWLEDGE or FIRST
BEAUTY   (see also BODY, CHARACTER, COVER-
       ING, MAKEUP, SEX, VISION)
  callisteia, callomania, kalon, kalopsia
BED   see SLEEP
BEGINNING   see FIRST
BEHAVIOR   see GOOD
BELIEF   (see also DECEPTION, KNOWLEDGE,
       REASON, RELIGION, RULE MAKER/RULE
       FOLLOWER, STRICTNESS, SUPERNATU-
       RAL, THOUGHT)
  adiabolism, agathism, cathexis, fideism, floromancy,

homo unius libri, idols of the theater, monism, mythomania, pancosmism, pelagianism, teleology, tranont

BELL   see SOUND

BIAS   see EQUALITY

BIBLE   see RELIGION

BIG   see LARGENESS

BIRTH   see CREATIVITY or CHILD

BITING   see MOUTH

BLEMISH   see WRINKLE

BLINDNESS   see VISION

BLOOD   (see also CONNECTION, CENTER,
      HEART, BODY)
   sphygmomanometer

BLOWING   see AIR

BODY   (see also BEAUTY, BONE, COVERING [AS
      IN CLOTHING], FACE, FEELING, FEET,
      HAIR, HAND, HEAD, HEART, ILLNESS/
      HEALTH, MAKEUP, MOUTH, NOSE, PAIN,
      SEX, SKIN, THROAT, TISSUE, WOUND,
      WRINKLE)
   agastopia, antipudic, artuate, embrocation, parenteral

BONE   (see also BODY, FOSSIL, SHELL, STONE)
   ossify

BOOK   see WORD

BOREDOM   see TIREDNESS

BORROWING   see GIVING

BOSS   see LEADER

BOWL   see PLATES AND PANS

BRANCH   see CONNECTION

BREAKING   see CUTTING

BREATHING   (see also AIR, NOSE)
   dyspnea

BRICK   see STONE

BRIGHTNESS   see LIGHT

BRISTLE   see HAIR

BROKEN   see CONNECTION

BROTHER   see FAMILY

BUGS   see INSECT

BUILDING   (see also CITY, HOME, SPACE, THING)
  petracide, tectonics

BULKY   see CARRY

BUREAUCRAT   see WORK

BURIAL   see DEATH

BURNING   see FIRE

BUTT   see TAIL

BUYING   see MONEY

CALM   see PEACE

CAPABILITY   see ABILITY

CARE   see LOVE

CARELESSNESS   see INDIFFERENCE

CARRY   (see also CARTS, DIRECTION, DROP,
    FEELING, HAND, PRESSURE, TRAVEL,
    WEIGHT)
  shlep, vade mecum

CART   (see also CARRY, VEHICLE)
  bollards, cartnapping

CAT   see ANIMAL

CAUSE/EFFECT   (see also CREATIVITY, EVENTS,
    KNOWLEDGE, PROBLEM, REASON,
    STRATEGY)
  acculturation, agathism, agnogenic, antistasis, chaogenous, eumoirous, homeopathy, idiopathic, mythopoeic, ylem

CELEBRATION   see EVENT

CELL   see NATURE

CENTER   (see also DIRECTION, POKING, WHEEL)
  cynosure
CERTAINTY   see KNOWLEDGE
CHANCE   see LUCK
CHANGE   see DIFFERENTNESS
CHAOS   see GOOD
CHARACTER   (see also BEAUTY, FEELING,
      LOVE/HATE, MAN/WOMAN, NATURE)
  atavistic, geloscopy, minimus, pathetic
  fallacy/anthropopathism, pelagianism, physiognomy,
  psilanthropism
CHEATING   see DECEPTION
CHESS   see PLAYING
CHEWING   see FOOD
CHILD   (see also ANIMALS, CREATIVITY, FAMILY,
      GROWTH, MARRIAGE, MAN/WOMAN, NA-
      TURE, SEX)
  afterages, anadramous, arrhenotoky, blithemeat, cou-
  vade, ephebic, hypocorism, kindergraph, meconium,
  nepimnemic, nidifugous, philoprogenitive/proletaneous,
  primipara, secundipara, unigeniture
CHIMES   see SOUND
CHOICES   see STRATEGY
CHOOSING   see STRATEGY
CHRISTIANITY   see RELIGION
CIGARETTES   see SMOKING
CIRCLE   see CENTER
CIRCULATION   see HEART
CITY   (see also BUILDINGS, COUNTRY, GOVERN-
      MENT, SPACES, WORLD)
  urbacity
CLARITY   see VISION
CLEANING   see DIRT

CLIMBING   see SUCCESS or WALKING or MOUN-
    TAINS
CLOSED   see OPEN
CLOSENESS   see CONNECTION
CLOTHING   see COVERING
CLOUD   see COVERING
COIN   see MONEY
COLD/HOT   (see also FIRE, LIGHT, SUN)
  eutexia
COLLECTION/COLLECTING   (see also CARRYING,
    HUNTING, WILLPOWER, VISION)
  bibliotaph, bumfodder, deltiology, receptary
COLOR   (see also FEELING, LIGHT, VISION)
  afterimage, chromatocracy, grisaille, isochromatic,
  miniate/rubricate, piebald, sematic
COMMUNICATION   see WORD or THOUGHT
COMPETITION   see PLAYING
COMPLAINT   see ARGUMENT
COMPLETENESS   see INCOMPLETENESS
COMPLIMENT   see PRAISE
COMPULSION   see WILLPOWER
COMPUTATION   see MATH
CONCEIT   see IMPORTANCE
CONCENTRATION   see THOUGHT
CONCERN   see INDIFFERENCE
CONCLUSION   see FIRST or REASON
CONCRETE   see ABSTRACT
CONFESSION/FORGIVENESS/REMORSE   (see   also
    GOOD/BAD, HAPPINESS/UNHAPPINESS, RE-
    LIGION)
  acceptilation, Canossa, jeofail, medela, peccavi
CONFIDENTIAL   see SECRECY
CONFUSION   see KNOWLEDGE

CONGRATULATION   see PRAISE

CONNECTION/GAP/LOSS   (see also BLOOD [AS IN CIRCULATION], CENTER, DEATH, FAMILY, FIRST, GOOD, MARRIAGE [AS IN WELL MATCHED], MEMORY, TIME)

accessit, coffle, imperdible, lacuna, osculant, pysma, stipple, sypher

CONTAINER   see COVERING

CONTAMINATION   see POISON

CONTROL/LACK OF CONTROL   see OPEN or WILLPOWER

CONVERSATION   see SPEAKING

COOKING   see FOOD

COUNTRY   (see also CITY, GOVERNMENT, NATURE, SPACE, WORLD)

autarky, cocarde, irredenta

COURT   see LAW

COVERING   (see also AIR [AS IN CLOUD], DECEPTION, HAPPINESS [AS IN CLOUD OF GLOOM], KNOWLEDGE/STUPIDITY, MAKEUP, OPEN/CLOSE, SECRECY, SHADOW, SHELL, SMOKING [AS IN SMOKE])

antipudic, cavernicolous, delaminate, embower, embrocation, immerge, inenubilable, mizzle/scud, serein, tare, tatterdemalion, ted

CRACK   see CONNECTION

CREATIVITY/NEWNESS   (see also ART, CAUSE/EFFECT, CHILD [AS IN BIRTH], FIRST, GROWTH, WORK, WRITING)

aha experience, handsel, logodaedalus, maieutic, misoneist, Newsthink, pygmalionism, tectonics

CRIME   (see also DECEPTION, FIGHTING, GIVING/TAKING, LAW, WAR)

coffle, embracery, hamesucken, suborn

CROWD   (see also FRIEND, ONE [AS IN ALONE
        AND AWAY FROM THE CROWD])
autophobia, ochlocracy, omnies

CULTURE   (see also ART, COUNTRY)
acculturation, irredenta

CURVING   see TURNING

CUTTING   (see also FIGHTING, HAIR, MEDICINE,
        NEEDLES, OPEN, POKING, SCRATCHING)
artuate, chaetophorous, delaminate, displume, exungulate, filtrate, hamble, interlucation, jugulate, microtome

DARK   see LIGHT

DART   see POKING

DATING   see LOVE

DAY   see TIME

DEADLINE   see TIME

DEATH   (see also CONNECTION, FIGHTING,
        FIRST, HELL, HUNTING, WAR, WASTE)
agonal, autophonomania, digamy, fetch light/corpse
candle, furfuration, infarct, muricide, oubliation,
petracide, philotheoparoptesism

DEBT   (see also GAMBLING, GIVING, MONEY)
acceptilation, expromission

DECEPTION   (see also ARGUMENT, BELIEF, COV-
        ERING, CRIME, EQUALITY/FAIRNESS/
        BIAS, GIVING/TAKING, GROWTH/
        DEFORMITY, HYPOCRISY, REASON/ILLOGIC,
        SECRECY/SURPRISE, SHADOW, VISION, YARN
        [AS IN TALL TALE, EXAGGERATED STORY])
accismus, anamorphosis, apistia, apophasis, Barmecidal, barnumize, bibliotaph, callomania, camouflet,

cockalorum, comprobatio, floccillation, kalopsia, kine-phantom, levant, machicolation, mahoitre, mycterism, mythomania, parhelion, pseudologue, pseudomnesia, reductive fallacy, sciamachy, suggestio falsi, thim-blerig, wordfact

DECISION   see STRATEGY

DECREASE   see NUMBER

DEED   see GOOD

DEFEATING   see SUCCESS

DEFECT   see GROWTH

DEFENSE   see WAR or ARGUMENT

DEFORMITY   see GROWTH

DEGREE   see LENGTH

DELAYING   see TIME

DELUSION   see DECEPTION

DEPENDENCE/INDEPENDENCE   (see also GIVING/
      TAKING, LEADER, LOVE/HATE, MARRIAGE,
      ONE [AS IN BY ONESELF, ON ONE'S OWN])
  autarky, heteronomous, monism

DEPRESSION   see HAPPINESS

DEPTH   see LENGTH

DESIRE   see WANT

DESTROYING   see FIGHTING

DESTRUCTION   see DEATH

DEVELOPMENT   see GROWTH

DIETING   see FOOD

DIFFERENTNESS/CHANGE/SAMENESS   (see also
      ARGUMENT, EQUALITY, GROWTH, OPPO-
      SITENESS, SPEED, STRATEGY, TURNING)
  aboiement, acculturation, allotheism, anamorphosis,
  anisosthenic, compeer, eclectic, equipotent, equiprobable, internecion, isochromatic, isochronal, mentimu-

tation, peripeteia, polylemma, skein, stereognosis, tranont, tropophobia, unasinous

DIFFICULTY   see ABILITY

DIMENSION   see LENGTH or LARGENESS

DINNER   see FOOD

DIRECTION   (see also CARRY, LEADER, POKING [AS IN POINTING], SPEED, STAR, SUCCESS [AS IN MOVING UPWARD], THOUGHT, THROWING, TRAVEL, TURNING)

aboral, anadramous, antisigogglin, peristalsis, rectigrade, reefer, sigogglin, sinistrodextral, winze

DIRT/CLEANING   (see also GOOD/BAD, LAND, POISON, SEX, WASTE)

amathophobia, bream

DISAGREEMENT   see ARGUMENT

DISAPPEARANCE   (see also DECEPTION, OPEN/ CLOSE, VISION)

virga

DISCHARGE   see THROWING

DISCOMFORT   see PAIN

DISCUSSION   see ARGUMENT

DISEASE   see ILLNESS

DISGUST   see LOVE

DISLIKE   see LOVE

DISORGANIZED   see GOOD

DISPLAY   see VISION

DISPUTE   see ARGUMENT

DISTANCE   see LENGTH

DISTORTION   see DECEPTION

DIVIDING   see CUTTING or TWO

DIVINE   see RELIGION

DIVORCE   see MARRIAGE

DOCTOR   see MEDICINE

DOCTRINE   see BELIEF
DOG   see ANIMAL
DOGMA   see BELIEF
DOLLAR   see MONEY
DOT   see SPOT
DOUBLE   see TWO
DOUBT   see KNOWLEDGE
DRAMA   (see   also   HAPPINESS/UNHAPPINESS,
    SHOW)
  bathos, peripeteia
DREAM   see SLEEP
DRESSING   see COVERING
DRINK   see LIQUID
DRIVING   see TRAVEL
DROP/DROPPING/DRIPPING   (see   also   CARRY,
    HANGING, NUMBER, SUCCESS)
  agroof, antipluvial, dogfall, furfuration, guttate, gutta-
  tim, kitchenstuff, recumbentibus, rhinorrhea, stillati-
  tious, virga
DUNG   see WASTE
DUPLICATION   see REPETITION
DURABILITY   see STRENGTH
DUST   see DIRT
DUTY   see WORK

EAR   see SOUND
EARTH   see WORLD
EASINESS   see ABILITY
EATING   see FOOD
EFFECT   see CAUSE
EFFORT   see WORK
EGOTISM   see IMPORTANCE
ELDERLY   see AGE

ELECTION   see LEADER
ELEMENT   see NATURE
EMBARRASSMENT   see CONFESSION
EMBLEM   see SYMBOL
EMOTION   see FEELING
EMPLOY   see WORK
EMPTY   see CONNECTION
ENCLOSURE   see COVERING
END   see FIRST or TAIL
ENEMY   see FIGHTING
ENTERTAINMENT   see SHOW
ENTRANCE   see OPEN
ENVIRONMENT   see WORLD
EQUALITY/FAIRNESS/BIAS   (see also DECEPTION,
     DIFFERENTNESS, GIVING, GOOD/BAD, LAW,
     LOVE, REASON/ILLOGIC)
  androlepsy, coparcener, idols of the cave, liberticidal,
  trim, usufruct
EQUALNESS (IN GENERAL)   see DIFFERENTNESS
ERASABLE   see OPEN
EROSION   see POKING
ERROR   see GOOD or KNOWLEDGE
ESCAPE   see OPEN
ETHNICITY   see SKIN or COLOR
EVENNESS   see EQUALITY or FLATNESS
EVENT   (see also CAUSE, NEWS, SHOW, TIME)
  antistasis, blithemeat, libation, pseudomnesia, skein
EVERYTHING   see WORLD
EVIDENCE   see INFORMATION
EVIL   see GOOD
EVOLUTION   see DIFFERENTNESS
EXCITEMENT   see HAPPINESS
EXCREMENT   see WASTE

EXCUSE   see REASON
EXISTENCE   see THING
EXIT   see OPEN
EXPLOSION   see THROWING
EYE   see VISION

FACE   (see also BEAUTY, DIRECTION, HEAD,
      MAKEUP, SIDE, WRINKLE)
  agroof, physiognomy, wog
FACT   see INFORMATION
FAILURE   see SUCCESS
FAIRNESS   see EQUALITY
FAITH   see BELIEF
FAITHFULNESS   see BELIEF
FALLACY   see ARGUMENT
FALLING   see SUCCESS or DROP
FALSITY   see DECEPTION
FAME   see SUCCESS
FAMILIARITY   see FRIEND
FAMILY   (see also ANIMAL, CHILD, GROWTH,
      HOME, MAN/WOMAN, MARRIAGE, SEX)
  atavistic, coparcener, dilling, epigone, genetic fallacy,
  oikonisus, uxorilocal
FANTASY   see DECEPTION
FARMING   see PLANT or ANIMAL
FASCINATION   see LOVE
FASTNESS   see SPEED
FAT   (see also LARGENESS)
  chubby chaser, kitchenstuff
FATHER   see MAN
FAVORITISM   see EQUALITY
FEAR   (see also HAPPINESS/UNHAPPINESS,
      INDIFFERENCE/OVERCONCERN, PRESSURE)

agowilt, agyiophobia, amathophobia, autophobia, cynophobia, ergasiophobia/ergophobia, homilophobia, keraunophobia, macrophobia, nucleomitophobia, rhytiphobia, topophobia, tropophobia

FEELING (see also BODY, CHARACTER [AS IN EMOTIONAL MAKEUP], COLOR, CREATIVITY, HAND, HAPPINESS/UNHAPPINESS, LOVE/HATE, MOUTH, NOSE, PAIN, PRESSURE, SEX, SMELL, SOUND, THOUGHT, VISION)

afterimage, aphilophrenia, cathexis, compathy, floromancy, mithridatism, pathetic fallacy/ anthropopathism, stereognosis

FEMALE   see MAN/WOMAN

FENCE   see OPEN

FIGHTING (see also ARGUMENT, CRIME, CUTTING, DEATH, HUNTING, LOVE, OPPOSITENESS, POKING, PUNISHMENT, SCRATCHING, STRENGTH, THROWING [AS IN EXPLODING/EXPLOSIVES], WAR)

arcifinious, armipotent, camouflet, cocarde, dogfall, flitwite, liberticidal, nucleomitophobia, philopolemical, phthisozoics, recumbentibus, sciamachy, sematic, sortie

FINGERS   see HAND

FIRE (see also COLD/HOT, LIGHT, SMOKING, SUN)

blype, ignivomous, joom

FIRST/LAST (see also CAUSE, CHILD [AS IN BIRTH], CONNECTION, CREATIVITY, DEATH, INCOMPLETENESS, LEADER/ LEADERSHIP, MOUTH [AS IN ENTRANCE

OR BEGINNING], NUMBER, ONE, SUC-
CESS, TAIL, TIME)

abecedarian, cena, genetic fallacy, paraph, prodromal,
serein, situs, tirocinium

FISH   see ANIMAL

FLAG   see SYMBOL

FLATNESS (see also PLATES AND PANS,
SCRATCHING [AS IN ERODING])

agroof, campestral, sypher

FLATTERY (see also DECEPTION, FRIEND,
LOVE)

elozable

FLEXIBILITY   see ABILITY or STRICTNESS

FLOWERS   see PLANT

FLYING   see AIR

FOOD (see also ANIMALS, GROCERY, GROWTH,
HUNTING, MOUTH, NATURE, OPEN/CLOSE
[AS IN DEVOURING], PLANT, PLATES AND
PANS, WASTE, WATER)

aristology, bever, blumba, bromatology, cena, commensal, convive, deipnosophist, geophagia/pica,
groaking, kitchenstuff, menstruum, pianteric, probang,
receptary, sitomania, tachyphagia, wog

FOOT (see also RUNNING, STANDING, TRAVEL,
WALKING)

cap-a-pie, dactylograde, digitigradient, discalceate,
grimpen, hamble, lassipedes, minimus, pedicab, savate

FOREST   see PLANT

FOREVER   see TIME

FORGETTING   see MEMORY or TIME

FORGIVING   see CONFESSION

FORM   see SHAPE

FOSSIL (see also AGE, BONE)

coprolite

FREEDOM   see WILLPOWER

FREEZING   see COLD

FRIEND/STRANGER   (see also CROWD, DIFFERENT-
    NESS/CHANGE, GIVING/TAKING, LOVE/HATE,
    MAN/WOMAN)

contesseration, convive, philoxenist

FRONT   see DIRECTION

FRUIT   see PLANT

FUNDAMENTAL   see KNOWLEDGE or FIRST

FUNNY   see LAUGHTER

GAMBLING   (see also DEBT, GIVING, MONEY)
  barato, levant

GAME   see PLAYING

GAP   see CONNECTION

GAWKING   see VISION

GENE   see FAMILY

GENITAL   see BODY

GHOST   see SUPERNATURAL

GIVING/TAKING   (see also CRIME, DEBT, DECEP-
    TION,   EQUALITY,   FIGHTING,   LOVE,
    MONEY, OPEN [AS IN REMOVE], PRAISE,
    WASTE)

callisteia, cartnapping, commensal, compathy, euphelicia, groaking, handsel, jerque, mactation, nostrificate,   parapherna,   philoxenist,   Pyrrhic   victory,
withernam

GOAL   see WANT

GOD   see RELIGION

GOLD   see MONEY

GOOD/BAD   (see   also   BEAUTY,   CHARACTER,
    CONFESSION / FORGIVENESS / REMORSE,

DIFFERENTNESS, DIRT, EQUALITY/
FAIRNESS/BIAS, FEELING, FIGHTING, FRIEND/
STRANGER, GIVING, GROWTH/DEFORMITY,
HAPPINESS/UNHAPPINESS, HEART, ILLNESS/
HEALTH, KNOWLEDGE/STUPIDITY, LAUGH-
TER, LENGTH/DEPTH [AS IN LOWNESS/EVIL],
LOVE/HATE, PAIN, POISON, RELIGION, SLEEP
[AS IN NIGHTMARES], SMELL [AS IN STENCH],
VOMIT)

acyrology, adiabolism, agathism, antistasis, blumba,
chaogenous, demimonde, eclectic, epinosic gain, eumoirous, eunomy, eusystolism, extradictionary, floromancy, kalon, medela, meed, mot juste, Newsthink,
noa, orthoepy, palinoia, paraphasia, peccavi, pelagianism, philippize, phthisozoics, quadriliteralism, rectigrade, redhibition, rhyparography, serendipitous, situs,
tacenda, tatterdemalion, vade mecum

GOSSIP   see SPEAKING

GOVERNMENT   (see also CITY, COUNTRY, CRIME,
LAW, LEADER/LEADERSHIP, RULE MAKER/
RULE FOLLOWER)

androcracy, androlepsy, chromatocracy, eunomy, gynarchy, irredenta, ochlocracy, panarchy, Pandemonium,
stratocracy, timocracy, troika

GRAMMAR   see WORDS

GRANDMOTHER   see FAMILY

GRATITUDE   see PRAISE

GRAVES   see DEATH

GREASE   (see also FOOD, WASTE)
kitchenstuff

GREATNESS   see   LARGNENESS

GREED   see GIVING

GROCERY   (see also FOOD)
   bodega, bollards, cartnapping
GROWTH/DEFORMITY   (see also AGE, ANIMAL,
      BODY, CHILD, CREATIVITY, DIFFERENTNESS/
      CHANGE,   FOOD,   GOOD,   HOME,   INSECT,
      KNOWLEDGE/STUPIDITY, MAN/WOMAN,
      PLANT, STRATEGY, TIME, TURNING,
      WRINKLE)
   accrescent, aerobic, campestral, cavernicolous, dehiscence, diastrophism, indehiscent, isauxesis, nit, photophobe, tachyauxesis
GULLIBILITY   see BELIEF

HABIT   see WILLPOWER
HAIR/HAIR-THIN   (see also CONNECTION, CUT-
      TING, LARGENESS/SMALLNESS, LENGTH,
      NEEDLE, ROD, YARN)
   chaetophorous, funicular, piloerection, vibrissae
HAND   (see also BODY, CARRYING, FEELING,
      POKING, SCRATCHING)
   dactylonomy, embrocation, fillip, grimpen, guddle,
   medius, minimus, onychophagy, savate, thimblerig,
   yepsen
HANGING   (see also CARRY, DIRECTION, DROPS,
      WEIGHT)
   filipendulous, funicular
HAPPINESS/UNHAPPINESS   (see also CONFESSION/
      FORGIVENESS/REMORSE, COVERING [AS
      IN CLOUD OF GLOOM], FEAR, FEELING,
      GOOD/BAD, ILLNESS/HEALTH, LOVE/HATE,
      PAIN, PEACE, RAIN [AS IN MISFORTUNE OR
      SADNESS],   SCRATCHING/TICKLING,   SEX,
      WAR)

anhedonia, autarchia, eristic, eumoirous, euneirophrenia, hedon, macarism, nikhedonia, polylemma, preterist, rhyparography, Schadenfreude

HARDNESS   see   STRENGTH

HARMFUL   see GOOD

HAT   see COVERING

HATE   see LOVE

HEAD   (see also FACE, THOUGHT)

cap-a-pie

HEALTH   see ILLNESS

HEARING   see SOUND

HEART   (see also BLOOD, BODY, CONNECTION, CENTER, LOVE)

cardiomegaly, memoriter, tachycardia

HEAT   see COLD or LIGHT or SUN

HEAVINESS   see WEIGHT

HEIGHT   see LENGTH

HELL   (see also PAIN, PUNISHMENT, RELIGION)

pandemonium

HESITATION   see SPEED

HIDING   see COVERING

HISTORY   see TIME

HITTING   see FIGHTING

HOLE   see SPACE

HOLINESS   see RELIGION

HOLLOW   see CONNECTION

HOME   (see also BUILDING, FAMILY, GROWTH, NATURE)

antiscians, arenicolous, cavernicolous, fimetarious, hamesucken, hibernaculum/hibernacle, lentic, nesiote, nidifugous, nostomania, outlier, sedentarize, urbacity, uxorilocal

HONESTY   see BELIEF

HONOR   (see also GIVING, PRAISE)
  displume, libation, timocracy
HOPE   see WANT
HOSPITAL   see MEDICINE
HOT   see COLD
HOUSE   see HOME
HUMAN   see MAN/WOMAN
HUMILIATION   see CONFESSION
HUMOR   see LAUGHTER
HUNTING   (see also ANIMAL, DEATH, DECEP-
        TION, DIRECTION, FOOD, KIDNAPPING,
        MINING, TRAVEL, VISION, WANT)
  hamble
HURT   see PAIN
HUSBAND   see MAN
HYPNOTISM   (see also MEMORY, WILLPOWER/
        COMPULSION/CONTROL)
  echolalus
HYPOCRISY   (see also DECEPTION)
  tu quoque/you-too-ism

IDEAS   see BELIEF or CREATIVITY
IDOLS   see RELIGION
IGNORANCE   see KNOWLEDGE
IGNORING   see INDIFFERENCE
ILLNESS/HEALTH   (see also BODY, FEELING,
        HAPPINESS/UNHAPPINESS, MEDICINE,
        PAIN, WOUND)
  epinosic gain, epiphenomenon, euphelicia, idiopathic,
  kinetosis, nosology, nosomania, pathocryptia, patho-
  dyxia, prodromal, prodrome
ILLOGIC   see REASON
ILLUSION   see DECEPTION

IMAGINATION   see CREATIVITY or DECEPTION
IMITATION   see REPETITION
IMMUNITY   see FEELING
IMPORTANCE/UNIMPORTANCE (see also INDIF-
      FERENCE/OVERCONCERN,   LARGENESS,
      LENGTH, NEEDLE [AS IN IMPORTANT
      POINT], THING, WEALTH, WEIGHT)
   ab irato, basilect, cathexis, cockalorum, cynosure,
   logomachy, militaster, minimus, morkrumbo, mungo,
   pedant, pettifogger, phrasemonger, psilosopher, scio-
   lism, sisyphean, sizzle seller
IMPOSSIBILITY   see REASON
IMPURITY   see POISON
INABILITY   see ABILITY
INCOMPLETENESS (see also FIRST/LAST,
      SUCCESS/FAILURE)
   abbozzo
INCREASE   see NUMBER
INDEPENDENCE   see DEPENDENCE
INDIFFERENCE/OVERCONCERN (see also FEAR,
      IMPORTANCE/UNIMPORTANCE, LOVE/
      HATE, SLEEP, STRICTNESS, THOUGHT,
      WANT, WILLPOWER, WORK)
   autophonomania, horaphthia, ideomania, kerdomeletia/
   plutomania, pathodyxia, rhytiscopia, sitomania
INFECTION   see POISON
INFERIORITY   see IMPORTANCE
INFLEXIBILITY   see STRICTNESS
INFORMATION (see also ARGUMENT, EVENT,
      KNOWLEDGE, MEMORY, NEWS, OPEN [AS
      IN OPEN MIND], QUESTION, SHOW,
      SPEAKING)

lacuna, Newsthink, Q.E.D., telepheme

INK   see WRITING

IN-LAWS   see FAMILY

INSECT (see also ANIMAL, LARGENESS/
        SMALLNESS, NATURE)
  frass, kermes, nit, ocelli

INSIGNIFICANCE   see IMPORTANCE

INSTRUCTION   see KNOWLEDGE

INSTRUMENT   see MEASUREMENT or SOUND

INSULT   see ARGUMENT

INTELLIGENCE   see KNOWLEDGE

INTERCOURSE   see SPEAKING or SEX

INTERPRETATION   (see also WORDS)
  anagoge

INTERRELATIONSHIP   see CONNECTION

INTRODUCTION   see FIRST

ISLAND   (see also LAND, ONE [AS IN ALONE],
        WATER)
  nesiote

JOINING   see CONNECTION

JUMPING   see TURNING

KEY   see OPEN

KIDNAPPING   (see also DECEPTION, HUNTING)
  androlepsy

KILLING   see DEATH

KINDNESS   see LOVE

KITCHEN   (see also FOOD, GROCERY, PLATES
        AND PANS)
  kitchenstuff

KNEES   see BODY

KNIVES   see CUTTING

KNOWLEDGE/STUPIDITY (see also ABILITY/
    INABILITY, ARGUMENT, BELIEFS, CAUSE,
    COVERING [AS IN CLOSED MIND],
    GROWTH, INFORMATION, INTERPRETA-
    TION, LIGHT, MEMORY, OPEN [AS IN OPEN
    MIND], PROBLEM, QUESTION, REASON/
    ILLOGIC, STRATEGY, TEACHING, TEST,
    THOUGHT, VISION)
abecedarian, ad ignorantiam, aegrotat, aha experience,
anoesis, areology/polemology, Boeotian, bottega, dactylonomy, didactic, echolalus, embolalia, epiplexis,
homo unius libri, idols of the cave, idols of the theater,
jeofail, logodaedalus, logodaedaly, maieutic, misotramontanism, opsimath, pedant, phronesis, polyhistorian/
polymath, psilosopher, psittacism, recension, receptary,
sciolism, sophophobia, unasinous

LACK see WEALTH
LAND (see also COUNTRY, DIRT, GROWTH,
    HOME, ISLAND, MOUNTAIN, NATURE,
    SPACE, WORLD)
campestral, diastrophism, glebe, mephitis, triphibious
LANGUAGE see SPEAKING
LARGENESS/SMALLNESS (see also FAT, HAIR/
    HAIR-THIN, IMPORTANCE, INSECT [AS IN
    TINY CREATURE], LENGTH, NUMBER,
    WEALTH)
bodega, cardiomegaly, cockalorum, delaminate, furfu-
ration, microtome, minimifidian, minimus, mithri-
datism, monticule, pianteric, Second Coming type
LAST see FIRST
LAUGHTER (see also HAPPINESS, WIT)
Abderian, gelastic, gelogenic, geloscopy, risibility

LAW (see also CRIME, EQUALITY, GOVERN-
   MENT, LEADER, RULE MAKER/RULE FOL-
   LOWER)
 barratry, heteronomous, jeofail, novation, pettifogger
LAZINESS   see TIREDNESS
LEADER/LEADERSHIP (see also DEPENDENCE,
   DIRECTION, FIRST, GOVERNMENT, RULE
   MAKER/RULE FOLLOWER)
 camarilla, compeer, demimonde, eyeservice, fugle-
 man, interpellation, menstruum, mésalliance/
 misalliance, militaster, morganatic
LEANING   see TURNING
LEARNING   see KNOWLEDGE
LEAVING   see OPEN
LEFT   see DIRECTION
LEGALITY   see LAW
LEGS   see BODY
LENGTH/DEPTH (see also GOOD/BAD [AS IN
   LOWNESS/EVIL], IMPORTANCE, LARGE-
   NESS, MOUNTAIN, SHAPE, TIME, WATER)
 ad libitum, aphelion, bathos, benthopelagic, bream,
 brevirostrate, eloign/eloin, ephemeromorph, laaba,
 mileway, ochlocracy, panchreston, scut, sound, tele-
 phanous
LETTER   see WORD or WRITING
LEVEL   see FLATNESS
LIBERTY   see EQUALITY
LIES   see DECEPTION
LIFT   see CARRY
LIGHT/DARK (see also COLOR, FEAR,
   KNOWLEDGE/STUPIDITY, SHADOW,
   STAR, SUN, VISION)
 advesperate, afterimage, aheliotropic, coruscation,

fetch light/corpse candle, interlucation, keraunophobia, photophobe

LIGHTNESS   see WEIGHT

LIKE   see LOVE

LIQUID   (see also ALCOHOL, DROP/DROPPING/
     DRIPPING, FOOD, WATER)

filtrate, libation, machicolation, slops

LIVING   see GROWTH

LOCATION   see SPACE

LOCKED   see OPEN

LOGIC   see REASON

LOOKING   see VISION

LOOSENESS   see STRENGTH

LOSING   see SUCCESS

LOSS   see CONNECTION

LOVE/HATE   (see also ARGUMENT, EQUALITY,
     FIGHTING, FRIEND, HAPPINESS, HEART,
     GIVING, GOOD, INDIFFERENCE, MAR-
     RIAGE, PRAISE, SEX)

ab irato, agastopia, allotheism, aphilophrenia, Boeotian, cachet, cathexis, chubby chaser, comprobatio,
cynophilist, epinosic gain, ergophile, extrapunitive,
hierofastidia, introjection, lexicomane, logofascinated,
logomisia, macarism, melomaniac, misogynist, misoneist, misotramontanism, mycterism, philogyny, philophronesis, philopolemical, philoprogenitive, pygmalionism, rhinestone vocabulary, sophophobia, suitorcide,
wordfact

LOWNESS   see LENGTH

LUCK   (see also GAMBLING, STRATEGY, SUCCESS,
     WILLPOWER/COMPULSION/CONTROL)

equiprobable, handsel

LUNCH   see FOOD

MAGAZINE   see WORD

MAKEUP   (see also BEAUTY, CHARACTER, COVERING, FACE, WRINKLE)

infucation

MALES   see MAN/WOMAN

MAN/WOMAN   (see also ANIMAL, CHARACTER, CHILD, FAMILY, GROWTH, HOME, MARRIAGE, NATURE, SEX)

androcracy, cinqasept, cockalorum, coffle, demimonde, gynarchy, lasslorn, misogynist, philogyny, spanogyny

MANURE   see WASTE

MAP   (see also DIRECTION, STRATEGY, WORLD)

uranography

MARRIAGE   (see also FAMILY, HOME, MAN/WOMAN, ONE [AS IN SINGLE], SEX)

apistia, apopemptoclinic, cicisbeo, digamy, dysonogamia, lairwite, mésalliance/misalliance, misogamy, morganatic, opsigamy, parapherna, schatchen

MATCHED (AS IN SUITABLE)   see GOOD

MATERIAL WORLD   see THINGS

MATHEMATICS   (see also MEASUREMENT, NUMBER)

dactylonomy

MEANING   see WORD

MEASUREMENT   (see also MATH, NUMBER, TEST)

algometer, algon, sphygmomanometer

MEDICINE   (see also BODY, ILLNESS/HEALTH, PAIN)

azoth/panpharmacon, cholelithotomy, ergasiophobia, homeopathy, nephrolithotomy, perissotomist, spansule

MELTING   see COLD

MEMORY   (see also CONNECTION, HYPNOTISM,
     INFORMATION, KNOWLEDGE, THOUGHT)
  lacuna, lethologica, lethonomia, memoriter, nepimne-
  mic, oofle, parapraxis, pseudomnesia, schizothemia,
  tintiddle
MESSY   see GOOD
METAL   (see also MINING)
  blumba
MILITARY   see WAR
MIMICKING   see REPETITION
MIND   see THOUGHT
MINING   (see also HUNTING, METAL, WANT [AS
     IN SEARCH])
  niter, winze
MINISTER   see RELIGION
MISSING   see CONNECTION
MISTAKE   see KNOWLEDGE
MOB   see CROWD
MONEY   (see also DEBT, GAMBLING, GIVING,
     WEALTH)
  chrysograph, emacity, embracery, flitwite, lairwite,
  levant, philippize, redhibition, sizzle seller, suborn,
  venditation, viaticum
MONSTER   see GOOD
MORALITY   see GOOD
MORNING   see TIME
MOTHER   see MAN/WOMAN
MOTION   see TURNING
MOUNTAIN   (see also COUNTRY, LAND, LENGTH/
     DEPTH, PROBLEM, STONE)
  alpinist, grimpen, monticule, ossa
MOURNING   see DEATH

MOUTH   (see also FOOD, OPEN/CLOSE, POKING, SPEAKING, WORD)
  gomphiasis, stomatic
MOVEMENT   see TURNING
MOVIES   (see also DRAMA, STAR, VISION)
  hiccup
MUSIC   see SOUND
MYTH   see KNOWLEDGE

NAIL   (see also NEEDLE/PIN, POKING)
  exungulate
NAME   (see also WORD)
  hypocorism, lethonomia, oofle
NATION   see COUNTRY
NATURE   (see also ANIMAL, CHARACTER, COUN-
      TRY, LAND, MAN/WOMAN, ONE, PLANT,
      SPACE, STAR, SUPERNATURAL, THING,
      WORLD)
  geophagia/pica, pathetic fallacy/anthropopathism, pe-
  lagianism, teleology
NAVY   see WAR
NEARNESS   see CONNECTION
NEEDLE/PIN   (see also HAIR, NAIL, POKING,
      YARN)
  acupinge, bodkin, gnomon
NEIGHBORS   see FRIEND
NEST   see HOME
NET   see CONNECTION
NEUTRALITY   see EQUALITY
NEVER   see TIME
NEWNESS   see CREATIVITY
NEWS   (see also EVENT, INFORMATION)
  reefer, Second Coming type

NEWSPAPER   see WORD

NIGHT   see TIME

NIGHTMARE   see SLEEP

NOISE   see SOUND

NOSE   (see also BREATHING, FEELING, SMELL, SNEEZING)

brevirostrate, rhinophonia, vibrissae

NUDITY   see COVERING

NUMBER   (see also AGE, CONNECTION, DROP, FIRST, LARGENESS, MATHEMATICS, MEASUREMENT, ONE, THREE, TWO, WEALTH)

ad libitum, allotropy, booby, factotum, philoprogenitive/proletaneous, spanogyny

NUTRITION   see FOOD

OATH   see CONFESSION

OBLIGATION   see WORK

OBSESSION   see INDIFFERENCE

OCEAN   see WATER

ODDNESS   see DIFFERENTNESS

ODOR   see SMELL

OFFICE   see WORK OR LEADER

OLD AGE   see AGE

ONE   (see also CROWDS, FIRST/LAST, ISLAND [AS IN ALONE], MARRIAGE [AS IN SINGLE], NUMBER, TWO)

holophrasis/holophrase/holophrasm, holus-bolus, monism, monoglot, polysemant, primipara, sortie, unigeniture, ylem

OPEN/CLOSE/PERMITTING/PROHIBITING   (see also COVERING, CUTTING, DECEPTION, DISAPPEARANCE, FOOD [AS IN SWALLOWING/DEVOURING], GIVING [AS IN REMOVING],

HUNTING [AS IN CAPTURING], KNOWL-
EDGE [AS IN OPEN MIND], TRAVEL [AS IN
ESCAPE], VISION)

adfenestrate, antistasis, arcifinious, bollards, grike,
guddle, hawk, indehiscent, interlucation, laaba, leeward, machicolation, panoptic, parenteral, petard,
probang, pseudothyrum, recrudescence, sudd, vibrissae

OPTION   see THOUGHT

OPPOSITENESS   (see also ARGUMENT, DIFFER-
ENTNESS, FIGHTING, TURNING)

antipodal, antiscians, countersuggestible

OPPOSITION   see FIGHTING

ORGANISM   see NATURE

ORIGIN   see FIRST

OVERATTENTION   see INDIFFERENCE

OVERCONCERN   see INDIFFERENCE

OVERSIMPLIFICATION   see DECEPTION

OWNERSHIP   see WEALTH

OXYGEN   see AIR

PADDING   see DECEPTION

PAIN   (see also BODY, CONFESSION/FORGIVENESS/
REMORSE, FEELING, FIGHTING, ILLNESS/
HEALTH, LOVE/HATE, MEDICINE, WOUND)

agonal, algometer, algon

PAINTING   (see also ART, PICTURE)

abbozzo, acupinge, bottega, grisaille, miniate/
rubricate, rhyparography, stipple

PAPER   (see also WRITING)

bumfodder, tare

PARENT   see FAMILY

PAYMENT   see MONEY

PEACE   (see also HAPPINESS/UNHAPPINESS,
      SOUND, WAR)
  calumet, commensal, irenic, lentic, philophronesis,
  soteria
PEOPLE see MAN/WOMAN
PERCEPTION   see FEELING
PERFECTION   see GOOD or STRICTNESS
PERMISSION   see OPEN
PERSUASION   see ARGUMENT
PHOBIA   see FEAR
PHOTOGRAPH   see PICTURE
PHRASE   see WORD
PICKING   see POKING
PICTURE   (see also ART, CULTURE, PAINTING,
      POSTCARD, STATUE, SYMBOL, WORD,
      WRITING)
  kindergraph
PIN   see NEEDLE
PITCH   see SOUND
PLACE   see WORLD
PLAN   see STRATEGY
PLANT   (see also FOOD, GROWTH, NATURE,
      WASTE)
  dendrochronology, echard, ephemeromorph, floro-
  mancy, holotype, interlucation, joom
PLATES AND PANS   (see also FLATNESS, FOOD,
      GROCERY)
  gnomon, yepsen
PLAYING   (see also STRATEGY, SHOW)
  booby, void, woodpusher
PLEASURE   see HAPPINESS
PLEDGE   see CONFESSION
POINTING   see POKING

POISON   (see also DIRT, GOOD/BAD, SMOKING)
  amathophobia, mithridate/treacle, mithridatism, se-
  matic
POKING/PRICKING/POINTING/BITING/PICKING
        (see also CENTER, CUTTING, DIRECTION,
        FIGHTING, MOUTH, NEEDLE, SCRATCH-
        ING)
  floccillation, onychophagy
POLITICS   see LEADER
POPULARITY   see CROWD
POSITION   see DIRECTION or SPACE
POSSESSION   see THING
POSSIBILITY   see DIFFERENTNESS or LUCK
POSTCARD   (see also PICTURE)
  deltiology
POVERTY   see WEALTH
PRACTICE   see REPETITION
PRAISE   (see also GIVING, HONOR, SPEAKING)
  comprobatio, macarism
PREACHING   see RELIGION
PRECISION   see STRICTNESS
PREJUDICE   see EQUALITY
PRESSURE   (see also CARRY, FEAR, WEIGHT)
  sphygmomanometer
PREVENTION   see OPEN
PRICKING   see POKING
PRIDE   (see also LOVE)
  urbacity
PRIVACY   see SECRECY
PRIZE   see GIVING
PROBABILITY   see LUCK
PROBLEM   (see also ABILITY, ARGUMENT,

KNOWLEDGE, MOUNTAIN, QUESTION, STRATEGY, THOUGHT)

aha experience, epiphenomenon, reductive fallacy

PRODUCTIVITY   see WORK
PROHIBITING   see OPEN
PRONUNCIATION   see SPEAKING
PROOF   see ARGUMENT
PROPERTY   see THING
PROSTITUTION   see SEX
PROTECTING   see OPEN
PUNISHMENT   (see also CONFESSION/FORGIVENESS/ REMORSE, DEATH, FIGHTING, HELL, WARN-ING/THREAT)

commination, epiplexis, withernam

PUPPET   (see also WILLPOWER/COMPULSION/ CONTROL)

galanty/mackninny

PURE   see CUTTING (AS IN UNCUT)
PURPOSE   see REASON
PURSUIT   see HUNTING
PUZZLE   see PLAYING

QUALIFIED   see ABILITY
QUANTITY   see NUMBER
QUESTION/ANSWER   (see also ARGUMENT, KNOWLEDGE, PROBLEM, REASON, STRATEGY, TEST, WORD)

camarilla, epiplexis, erotesis, hypophora, pysma

RACE   see SKIN or COLORS
RADIO   see SHOW
RAGGED   see GOOD
RAIN   (see also DROP, WATER)

brash/spate, mizzle/scud, serein, virga

RANK   see LEADER

READING   (see also VISION, WORD, WRITING)
bibliobibuli, lection

REALITY   see THING

REASON/ILLOGIC   (see also ARGUMENT, BELIEF,
CAUSE, COVERING [AS IN OPEN MIND],
DECEPTION, KNOWLEDGE/STUPIDITY,
OPEN [AS IN OPEN MIND], PROBLEM,
QUESTION, STRATEGY, THOUGHT)
aegrotat, dichaeologia, fideism, hypophora, misology,
mythoclast, mythopoeic, nosomania, paralogize, ris-
ibility, sophistry

RECIPE   see FOOD

REJECTION   (see also TURNING)
lasslorn

RELATEDNESS   see CONNECTION, FAMILY

RELIGION   (see also BELIEF, CONFESSION, GOOD/
BAD, HELL, LOVE/HATE, SUPERNATURAL)
allotheism, commination, glebe, hierofastidia, homilophobia, lection, philotheoparoptesism, psilanthropism

REMORSE   see CONFESSION

REMOVAL   see OPEN

REPETITION/DUPLICATION   (see also RETURN-
ING,   SUBSTITUTION,   TWO   [AS   IN
DOUBLE], WORK)
couvade, dittography, echolalus, holotype, hypocorism,
latah, miryachit, palinoia, psittacism, verbigeration

REPLY   see QUESTION

REPRESSION   see OPEN

REQUEST   see QUESTION

RESIDENCE   see HOME

RESPECT   see LOVE

RESPONSE   see QUESTION

RESPONSIBILITY   see WORK

RESTRICTION   see LAW or OPEN

RESULT   see CAUSE

RETURNING   (see also REPETITION, TRAVEL, TURNING)

  nostomania, redhibition

REVENGE   see PUNISHMENT

REVERSAL   see TURNING

REWARD   see MONEY or HONOR

RHYTHM   see TIME or SOUND

RICHNESS   see WEALTH

RIDGE   see WRINKLES

RIGHT   see DIRECTION

RIGHTS   see EQUALITY

RINGING   see SOUND

ROAD   (see also TRAVEL, VEHICLE, WHEEL)

  agyiophobia, jehu

ROCK   see STONE

ROD   (see also HAIR, LENGTH, NEEDLE)

  probang

ROLLING   see TURNING

ROMANCE   see LOVE

ROPE   see HAIR

ROUND   see WHEEL

RUBBING   see HAND

RULE MAKER /RULE FOLLOWER   (see also BELIEF, DEBT, GOVERNMENT, LAW, LEADER/LEADERSHIP, STRICTNESS, WORK)

  dixit, heteronomous, logogogue, pedant, pro forma

RUNNING   (see also FOOT, OPEN/CLOSE [AS IN ESCAPING], TRAVEL, WALKING)

  levant, rhinorrhea

SACRIFICE   see GIVING

SADNESS   see HAPPINESS

SAILING   see SHIP

SALAD   see FOOD

SALE   see MONEY

SAMENESS   see DIFFERENTNESS

SAND   (see also DIRT, STONES, WATER)
  arenicolous

SATISFACTION   see HAPPINESS

SAVING   see WASTE or MONEY

SAWING   see CUTTING

SCAB   see WOUND

SCARCITY   see NUMBER

SCRATCHING/TICKLING   (see also CUTTING,
        FEELING, HAND, POKING, WOUND)
  gargalesthesia

SEAL   see SYMBOL

SEARCHING   see VISION

SEASON   see TIME

SECRECY/SECRET/SURPRISE   (see also DECEP-
        TION, OPEN/CLOSE)
  agnogenic, argot, brash/spate, camarilla, demimonde,
  peculium, pseudothyrum, succubus

SEEING   see VISION

SELF-DECEPTION   see DECEPTION

SELF-SUFFICIENCY   see DEPENDENCE

SELFISHNESS   see GIVING

SELLING   see MONEY

SENSE (AS IN COMMON SENSE)   see KNOWL-
        EDGE

SENSE   see FEELING

SERIOUSNESS   see IMPORTANCE

SERMON   see RELIGION

SEX   (see also BODY, CONNECTION, CREATIV-
       ITY, DIRT, FAMILY, MAN/WOMAN, MAR-
       RIAGE)
   anililagnia, brocage, melolagnia, O.S.S., uxorovalence
SHADOW   (see also COVERING, DECEPTION,
       LIGHT/DARK, SUN)
   antiscians, gnomon
SHAPE   (see also LARGENESS, LENGTH/DEPTH)
   allotrope, allotropy, anamorphosis, pro forma,
   stereognosis
SHARING   see GIVING
SHARP   see POKING
SHAVING   see CUTTING
SHELL   (see also BONE, COVERING, FOSSIL,
       STONE, STRENGTH [AS IN HARDNESS])
   obtected
SHIP   (see also TRAVEL, WAR [AS IN NAVY],
       WATER)
   bream
SHOOTING   see FIGHTING
SHORTNESS   see LENGTH
SHOULDER   (see also BODY)
   mahoitre
SHOW   (see also DRAMA, EVENT, INFORMATION,
       PLAYING)
   hammocking
SIBLING   see FAMILY
SICKNESS   see ILLNESS
SIDE   (see also DIRECTION)
   antipodal
SIGHT   see VISION
SILENCE   see SOUND
SIMILARITY   see DIFFERENTNESS

SIN   see GOOD

SINGLE   see MARRIAGE (AS IN UNMARRIED)

SISTER   see FAMILY

SIZE   see LARGENESS

SKILL   see ABILITY

SKIN   (see also BEAUTY, BODY, FEELING, MAKEUP, SEX, WOUND, WRINKLE)
  blype, chromatocracy, furfuration, irredenta

SKY   see AIR

SLEEP   (see also GOOD/BAD [AS IN NIGHTMARE], INDIFFERENCE, TIREDNESS, WANT [AS IN DREAM], WORK)
  diurnation, euneirophrenia, outlier, somniloquism, succubus

SLIPPERINESS   see CARRYING

SLOWNESS   see SPEED

SMALLNESS   see LARGENESS

SMELL   (see also AIR, BREATHING, FEELING, GOOD/BAD [AS IN STENCH], NOSE)
  mephitis, olid

SMOKING   (see also AIR, FIRE, POISON)
  calumet, divan, fumacious

SMOOTHNESS   see FLATNESS or ABILITY

SNEEZING   (see also NOSE, THROWING)
  sternutation

SNOBBISHNESS   see IMPORTANCE

SOCIAL STATUS   see LEADER

SOLUTIONS   see KNOWLEDGE

SOUND   (see also FEELING, PEACE)
  aboiement, auscultate, cedilla, keraunophobia, melolagnia, melomaniac, omnies, sound, sternutation, tinnitus

SPACE (see also BUILDING, COUNTRY, LAND, NATURE, WORLD)

agate, bottega, bilocation, divan, situs, topopolitan, void

SPEAKING (see also ARGUMENT, CONFESSION, DECEPTION, INFORMATION, PRAISE, SOUND, THROAT, WORD, WRITING)

accismus, acyrology, anacoluthon, argot, aristology, basilect, deipnosophist, dixit, embolalia, homilophobia, idiolalia, latah, miryachit, monoglot, monology, musculade, mythomania, orthoepy, paraphasia, parapraxis, pathocryptia, pathodyxia, peccavi, philippize, philophronesis, phrasemonger, psittacism, rhinestone vocabulary, rhinophonia, schesis, slurvian, somniloquism, suggestio falsi, tacenda, telepheme, tintiddle, topophobia, tranont

SPEED (see also DIFFERENTNESS/CHANGE, DIRECTION, TIME, TRAVEL)

agyiophobia, isauxesis, kinephantom, tachyauxesis, tachycardia, tachydidaxy, tachyphagia

SPELLING see WORD

SPEWING see THROWING

SPLITTING see CUTTING

SPOILED see WANT

SPOT (see also WOUND)

guttate, ophthalmospintherism, piebald, stipple

SPREADING see COVERING

STAGE see DRAMA

STAMP see SYMBOL

STANDING (see also FOOT, RUNNING, WALKING)

macrophobia

STAR (see also AIR, LIGHT, MOVIES, NATURE, SUCCESS, SUN, WORLD) uranography

STATUE (see also ART, PAINTING, PICTURE)
effigiate

STATUS see LEADER

STEALING see GIVING

STIMULATION see FEELING

STING see POKING

STOCK see MONEY

STONE (see also ABSTRACT/CONCRETE, BUILD-
ING, FOSSIL, MOUNTAIN, SAND, SHELL,
STRENGTH [AS IN HARDNESS], STRICT-
NESS [AS IN HARDNESS])

cholelithotomy, lapidate, machicolation, nephrolithotomy, petracide

STOPPAGE see OPEN

STRAIGHTNESS see DIRECTION or GOOD

STRANGER see FRIEND

STRATEGY (see also LUCK, MAP, PLAYING,
QUESTION, REASON, SUCCESS, TEST,
TRAVEL [AS IN PURSUIT], WANT, WILL-
POWER)

eclectic, mentimutation, oofle, polylemma, teleology,
thimblerig, tropophobia

STREET see ROAD

STRENGTH/WEAKNESS (see also ILLNESS, IM-
PORTANCE, LARGENESS, SHELL [AS IN
HARDNESS], TIREDNESS)

anisosthenic, armipotent, equipotent, gomphiasis, olid

STRICTNESS (see also BELIEF, INDIFFERENCE/
OVERCONCERN, NEEDLE [AS IN POINTED,
DIRECT, PRECISE], RULE MAKER/RULE
FOLLOWER, STONE [AS IN HARD/
UNCHANGING])

ossify

STRING   see YARN
STUDENT   see KNOWLEDGE
STUPIDITY   see KNOWLEDGE
SUBSTITUTION   (see also DIFFERENTNESS/
      CHANGE, REPETITION)
  novation
SUCCESS/FAILURE   (see also ARGUMENT, DEATH,
      DIRECTION, FIGHTING, FIRST, GROWTH,
      LUCK, STAR [AS IN FAME], WAR [AS IN
      WINNING A WAR], WEALTH)
  accessit, barato, callisteia, dichaeologia, florescence,
  hammocking, nikhedonia, Pyrrhic victory, Schaden-
  freude, suitorcide
SUGAR   see FOOD
SUICIDE   see DEATH
SUIT   see LAW
SUITABILITY   see GOOD
SUN   (see also AIR, COLD/HOT, COLORS, COVER-
      ING, FIRE, LIGHT, STAR, VISION)
  aphelion, blype, gnomon, immerge, parhelion, serein
SUPERNATURAL   (see also BELIEF, NATURE, RE-
      LIGION)
  anagoge, succubus
SURGERY   see MEDICINE
SURPRISE   see SECRECY
SWIMMING   see WATER
SWITCHING   see SUBSTITUTION
SYMBOL   (see also ART, PICTURE, WORD)
  blumba, cachet, cocarde, paraph

TAIL   (see also FIRST/LAST)
  caudal, pygalgia, scut
TAKING   see GIVING

TALKING   see SPEAKING

TALLNESS   see LENGTH

TEACHING   (see also KNOWLEDGE)
  heuristics, tachydidaxy

TEARDROP   see WATER

TEARING   see CUTTING

TELEVISION   see SHOW

TEST   (see also KNOWLEDGE, MEASUREMENT,
      PROBLEM, QUESTION, REASON)
  auscultate, heft, invigilate, sound

THANKS   see PRAISE

THEATER   see DRAMA

THEFT   see GIVING

THEOLOGY   see RELIGION

THEORY   see BELIEF

THING/REALITY   (see also IMPORTANCE, NA-
      TURE, ONE, WEALTH, WORLD, names of
      particular things)
  bibliobibuli, jerque, kerdomeletia, menstruum, monism, mungo, pancosmism, usufruct, viaticum

THINNESS   see LARGENESS or HAIR

THOUGHT   (see also ARGUMENT, BELIEF, COV-
      ERING [AS IN OPEN MIND], DIRECTION,
      FEELING, HEAD, INDIFFERENCE/OVER-
      CONCERN, KNOWLEDGE, MEMORY, OPEN
      [AS IN OPEN MIND], PROBLEM, QUES-
      TION, REASON, SPEED, STRATEGY)
  cathexis, hypoprosexia, ideomania, mentimutation

THREAD   see YARN

THREAT   see WARNING

THREE   (see also NUMBER)
  pedicab, troika

THROAT   (see also BODY, SPEAKING)
  gargalesthesia, hawk, jugulate
THROWING   (see also DIRECTION, FIGHTING,
      SNEEZING, TRAVEL)
  dehiscence, gnomon, ignivomous, introjection, jettison, lapidate, meconium, niter, petard
THUNDER   see SOUND
TICKLING   see SCRATCHING
TILTING   see TURNING
TIME   (see also AGE, CAUSE/EFFECT, CONNEC-
      TION, EVENT, FIRST, LENGTH, MEMORY,
      NEWS, SPEED)
  ad libitum, advesperate, atavistic, autarchia, biduous,
  bilocation, brash/spate, cinqasept, diurnation, dysrhythmia, florescence, fortnight, gnomon, hebdomadal, hibernaculum/hibernacle, holus-bolus, hypo-
  prosexia, idols of the theater, irredenta, isochronal,
  jornada, menstruum, mileway, nudiustertian/pridian, per-
  noctation, preterist, recrudescence, schizothemia, si-
  syphean, spansule, sudd, thestreen, yestreen
TIREDNESS   (see also SLEEP, STRENGTH/WEAK-
      NESS, WORK)
  dysrhythmia, lassipedes, pandiculation
TISSUE   (see also BODY)
  infarct, microtome
TOBACCO   see SMOKING
TOE   see FOOT
TOMORROW   see TIME
TONGUE   see MOUTH
TOOTH   see MOUTH
TOUCH   see FEELING
TRACK   see HUNTING
TRAIL   see HUNTING

TRANSPORTATION   see VEHICLE

TRAP   see OPEN

TRAVEL   (see also AIRPLANE, CARRY, CART, DI-
RECTION, DROP, FOOT, OPEN/CLOSE [AS
IN ESCAPING], RETURNING, ROAD, RUN-
NING, SHIP, SPEED, STAR [AS FOR DIREC-
TION], STRATEGY [AS IN PURSUIT],
VEHICLES, VISIT, WALKING, WHEEL)
jornada, sedentarize, viaticum

TREE   see PLANT

TRICKERY   see DECEPTION

TRIVIA   see IMPORTANCE

TRUTH   see REASON

TURNING   (see also DIFFERENTNESS/CHANGE,
DIRECTION, GROWTH, RETURNING)
aheliotropic, bathos, evert, fillip, kinephantom, kinetosis, ossa, photophobe, sigogglin, skein

TWISTING   see TURNING

TWO   (see also NUMBER, REPETITION)
biduous, bilocation, digamy, diplopia, fortnight, secundipara

UGLY   see GOOD

UNCERTAINTY   see KNOWLEDGE

UNDERGROUND   see LENGTH

UNDRESSING   see COVERING

UNEXPECTEDNESS   see SECRECY

UNHAPPINESS   see HAPPINESS

UNION   see CONNECTION/GAP

UNIMPORTANCE   see IMPORTANCE

UNIQUENESS   see ONE

UNIVERSE   see WORLD

UNKNOWN   see CONNECTION or KNOWLEDGE

UNLOCKED   see OPEN
UNMARRIED   see MARRIAGE
UNORGANIZED   see GOOD
UPSIDE DOWN   see TURNING

VANITY   (see also BEAUTY, INDIFFERENCE/
      OVERCONCERN)
   elozable, pygmalionism
VARIATION   see DIFFERENTNESS
VEGETABLE   see PLANT
VEHICLE   (see also AIRPLANE, CART, DIREC-
      TION, ROAD, SHIP, SPEED, TRAVEL,
      WHEEL)
   pedicab, tare
VICTORY   see SUCCESS
VISION   (see also COLOR, COVERING, DECEP-
      TION, DISAPPEARANCE, EQUALITY/
      FAIRNESS/BIAS [AS IN BLINDNESS OR
      LACK OF BLINDNESS], FEELING, HUNT-
      ING, KNOWLEDGE, LIGHT, MOVIE,
      OPEN/CLOSE, READING, SECRECY, SUN,
      WANT, WINDOW)
   anamorphosis, cynosure, diplopia, floccillation, groaking, invigilate, jerque, microtome, ocelli, ophthalmospintherism, opsablepsia, panoptic, pro forma, Q.E.D.,
   serendipitous, strabismus, telephanous, venditation
VISIT   (see also TRAVEL)
   cinqasept
VOICE   see SPEAKING
VOMIT   (see also GOOD/BAD, WASTE)
   ignivomous

WAITING   see TIME

WALKING   (see also FOOT, RUNNING, STANDING,
        TRAVEL)
  agyiophobia, alpinist, grimpen, mileway
WALLS   see OPEN
WANDER   see TRAVEL
WANT   (see also INDIFFERENCE, SLEEP [AS IN
        DREAM], STRATEGY, TRAVEL [AS IN PUR-
        SUIT], WEALTH/POVERTY, WILLPOWER,
        WORK)
  accismus, aphilophrenia, euphelicia, groaking, oikonisus,
  phronesis, pica, serendipitous
WAR   (see also CRIME, DEATH, FIGHTING,
        PEACE, SHIP, SUCCESS/FAILURE, THROW-
        ING [AS IN EXPLOSION], WASTE)
  areology/polemology, logomachy, militaster, myrmidon/
  pandour, philopolemical, stratocracy, tirocinium
WARNING/THREAT   (see also ARGUMENT, FIGHT-
        ING, PUNISHMENT)
  commination, prodrome, sematic
WASTE   (see also DIRT, FOOD, GIVING, MONEY,
        WORK)
  bumfodder, coprolite, fimetarious/fimicolous, frass,
  kitchenstuff, meconium, mungo, peristalsis, slops, ted
WATER   (see also AIR, DROP/DROPPING/
        DRIPPING, FOOD, ISLAND, LAND,
        LENGTH/DEPTH [AS IN OCEAN DEPTH],
        LIQUID, RAIN, SHIP)
  anadramous, benthopelagic, echard, jettison, oubliation, sudd, triphibious
WEAKNESS   see STRENGTH
WEALTH/POVERTY   (see also IMPORTANCE,
        MONEY, NUMBER, SUCCESS, THING,
        WANT)

armentose, Barmecidal, kerdomeletia/plutomania, peculium, pelf, soteria, usance

WEAPON   see FIGHTING

WEB   see CONNECTION

WEEK   see TIME

WEIGHT   (see also CARRY, FAT, HANGING, IMPORTANCE/UNIMPORTANCE, LARGENESS/SMALLNESS, PRESSURE)
baraesthesia, baric, heft, stereognosis, tare

WHEEL   (see also ROAD, TRAVEL, VEHICLE)
trochal

WHISPERING   see SPEAKING

WIDTH   see LENGTH

WIFE   see MAN/WOMAN

WILLPOWER/COMPULSION/CONTROL   (see also ALCOHOL [AS IN ALCOHOLISM AND LACK OF WILLPOWER OR CONTROL], HYPNOTISM, INDIFFERENCE/OVERCONCERN, PUPPET, WANT)
aboiement, anoesis, dittography, echolalus, emacity, fumacious, latah, nostomania, palinoia, paraphasia, parapraxis, pathocryptia, pseudologue

WIND   see AIR

WINDOW   (see also OPEN/CLOSE, VISION)
adfenestrate

WINNING   see SUCCESS

WINTER   see TIME

WISDOM   see KNOWLEDGE

WISH   see WANT

WIT   (see also ABILITY, KNOWLEDGE, LAUGHTER)
coruscation, tintiddle

WITCH   see SUPERNATURAL

WOMAN   see MAN/WOMAN

WORDS   (see also ARGUMENT, FEELING, INFOR-
MATION, INTERPRETATION, NAME, QUES-
TION, READING, SPEAKING, SYMBOL,
WRITING)

aphasia, bibliotaph, definiendum, dittography, eusystolism, extradictionary, homo unius libri, lethologica,
lexicomane, logodaedalus, logofascinated, logogogue,
logomachy, logomisia, miniate/rubricate, mot juste,
mycterism, noa, noun-banging/nounspeak, O.S.S.,
pandect, polygraphy, polysemant, polysemy, pseudologue, quadriliteralism, reefer, Second Coming type,
verbigeration, wordfact

WORK   (see also CREATIVITY, INDIFFERENCE,
REPETITION, RULE MAKER/RULE FOL-
LOWER, SLEEP, TIREDNESS, WANT,
WASTE, WILLPOWER)

ergasiophobia/ergophile, ergophobe, eyeservice, factotum, introjection, morkrumbo, outlier, polygraphy,
sisyphean

WORLD/EVERYTHING   (see also ANIMAL, COUN-
TRY, LAND, MAN/WOMAN, NATURE, ONE,
PLANT, SPACE, STAR, SUPERNATURAL,
THING/REALITY)

agathism, azoth/panpharmacon, cap-a-pie, holus-
bolus, panarchy, pandect, ylem

WORRY   see FEAR

WORSHIP   see LOVE or RELIGION

WORTH   see IMPORTANCE

WOUND   (see also FIGHTING, POKING, PROB-
LEM, SCRATCHING, WRINKLE)

cicatrix, recrudescence

WRESTLING   see FIGHTING

WRINKLE   (see also AGE, FACE, GROWTH/
      DEFORMITY, MAKEUP, PROBLEMS,
      WOUND)
   dendrochronology, rhytiphobia, rhytiscopia
WRITING   (see also ART, PAPER, PICTURE, READ-
      ING, SPEAKING, SYMBOL, WORD)
   abbozzo, aegrotat, agonal, bathos, Boeotian, bromatology, chrysograph, epistolary, palimpsest, paraph,
   peripeteia, recension, rhyparography, vade mecum

YARN   (see also DECEPTION [AS IN TALL TALE/
      EXAGGERATED STORY], HAIRS, NEEDLE)
   filipendulous
YESTERDAY   see TIME
YOUNG   see AGE, CHILD